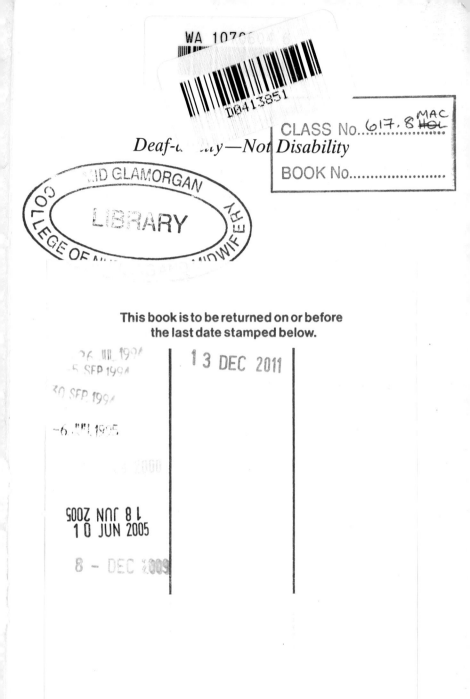

Deaf-u... ...y—Not Disability

**This book is to be returned on or before
the last date stamped below.**

Please contact us for the latest book information:
Multilingual Matters Ltd,
Bank House, 8a Hill Road,
Clevedon, Avon BS21 7HH,
England.

Deaf-ability—Not Disability:

A Guide for the Parents of Hearing Impaired Children

Wendy McCracken and
Hilary Sutherland

*With a Foreword by
Her Royal Highness
The Princess of Wales*

MULTILINGUAL MATTERS LTD
Clevedon • Philadelphia • Adelaide

To Jim

Library of Congress Cataloging in Publication Data

McCracken, Wendy, 1952–
Deaf-Ability, Not Disability: A Guide for the Parents of Hearing
Impaired Children/Wendy McCracken and Hilary Sutherland.
p. cm.
Includes bibliographical references and index.
1. Parents of Handicapped Children. 2. Child Rearing.
3. Children, Deaf – Family Relationships. 4. Hearing Impaired
Children – Family Relationships.
I. Sutherland, Hilary, 1955– . II. Title.
HO759.913.M33   1991
649.1512   dc20.

British Library Cataloguing in Publication Data

A CIP catalogue record for this book is available from the British Library.

ISBN 1-85359-081-9
ISBN 1-85359-080-0 (pbk)

Multilingual Matters Ltd

UK: Bank House, 8a Hill Road, Clevedon, Avon BS21 7HH, England.
USA: 1900 Frost Road, Suite 101, Bristol, PA 19007, USA.
Australia: PO Box 6025, 83 Gilles Street, Adelaide, SA 5000, Australia.

Copyright © 1991 Wendy McCracken & Hilary Sutherland.

Typeset by Wayside Books, Clevedon.
Printed and bound in Great Britain by Billing & Sons Ltd.

Contents

KENSINGTON PALACE

From my experience as Patron of the British Deaf Association, I know that deafness is still widely misunderstood. When parents are informed that their child has a hearing loss the future can seem bleak and frightening. This book has been written specifically for parents and others concerned with the care of hearing-impaired children. The individuals' stories which it relates challenge preconceptions about the treatment of all handicapped children. I hope that the struggles and triumphs described here will remind parents of the simple needs shared by every child for love, care and encouragement.

In seeking to dispel prejudice and underline the potential of all hearing-impaired children, the authors (one deaf and one hearing) advance a vital cause that I am delighted to support.

November 1990

Introduction

The aim of this book is to help parents of hearing impaired children, their families and interested professionals. It is mostly other people's attitudes that limit hearing impaired children. We put limits on them. By learning about deafness one can break down fears, dispel worries, learn, understand and take charge.

We set out with two shared ideas. Firstly, all children, although they may have a label of deafness, are above all else children; as such they deserve love, understanding and nurture. Secondly, parents need access to detailed unbiased information that enables them to make informed decisions regarding their own children. With these two beliefs we set out to write this book.

Our starting points were quite different. Hilary is a severely deaf mother with a profoundly deaf son; Wendy is a teacher of the deaf and an audiologist: practical experience and theory together. We have both seen and experienced the shock and devastation that diagnosis of deafness can bring to families. Fear of the unknown is very powerful. It is important to stress that your child is the same child before and after diagnosis. There will be many questions, concerns and worries. Give yourself some time, enjoy your child. Certainly ask questions and seek advice when you need to. This book will provide basic information and give some practical ideas about hearing impairment.

There is a mass of information for parents to digest. Treat this book as you would a large picnic. Pick out sections which interest you and are relevant to your present needs. Sample the case studies; they offer a rich and varied account of families and individuals. If one area seems to be too heavy give yourself a chance, take it slowly, re-read. We feel sure the end product is worth the effort: we know that hearing impaired children are.

Our work on this book has taught us much. We have both modified our views, challenged old prejudices, learned to listen more and to value widely differing opinions. There is no one answer, no right and wrong. There are many approaches which meet a variety of needs presented by hearing impaired children. No one person has all the answers. This book is a starting point for those involved with hearing impaired children; beyond it lies an exciting world. Every child has abilities and potential which you can help them to develop.

Hilary Sutherland
Wendy McCracken

Acknowledgements

It is impossible to thank everyone individually, so many people have helped make this book possible. Our particular thanks go to all the families and individuals who contributed their stories. The lovely photographs have been kindly provided by the National Deaf Children's Society, Breakthrough Trust, National Aural Group and their photographer Mr M. Gould, A.B.I.P.P. of the Photographic Department at Warwick University, and finally Liz Hurst of the Medical Illustrations Department at the Bristol Royal Infirmary. We would also like to thank Ian Funnel, the B.D.A. cartoonist, for allowing us to use his work.

Many friends have offered support over two years; in particular thanks should go to Paul, Sara and Jane. Thanks also to Jim for his help with the computer and Bev for his help with the text. Our families have offered us patience, support and encouragement and borne the brunt of disruption: we are especially grateful to them.

Part I

CHAPTER 1
Diagnosis

The test which shows that your child has a marked hearing loss, is partially hearing or profoundly deaf will change your life. It is unlikely that parents will ever forget the moment that deafness was diagnosed, but the rush of emotions which follows does make it hard for them to take in the other information that will be given at the time. As a result of this parents often have very negative feelings about the diagnosis and the way it was handled. Unfortunately, parents may also have to cope with unsympathetic professionals who deal with hearing impaired children daily and can easily forget the impact on the family of being told their child is deaf. One grandmother wrote: 'My daughter's situation would have been helped if there had been more co-operation between the professionals, perhaps more sensitivity to the traumatic experience, particularly at the time of diagnosis'. Sometimes the words which are used to explain the degree of hearing loss only serve to confuse parents further, as in this case: '"Lots of useful hearing" sounded great to me, then I found out that it meant he could be helped by a hearing aid, not that he had normal hearing'. In some cases the hearing loss may be confused with other problems, especially if a child has an obvious physical or mental disability. In the following example there were other problems and the child in question was not finally diagnosed as being severely deaf until she was seven:

> They said she was an uncommunicative child, well deaf children do tend to be! She just stared at everyone. She got bored with repeating the tests again and again. She was a good lip-reader and had some useful hearing so she did respond on some occasions, they couldn't sort it all out.

When your child is found to have a hearing loss you will have lots of questions that you have never faced before. How do they know he is deaf? What does 'deaf' mean? Will an operation help?

3

Can my child hear anything at all? Will he always be deaf? What
about these cures I have read about in the paper? Why should my
child have to be singled out? How will I know what to do? The list
of questions is almost endless; as one question is answered another
will replace it. The Ear, Nose and Throat consultant, audiologist
and the teacher of the deaf will all offer answers and information
in the early stages and much of this will simply be lost as parents
start to cope with the new idea — that they have a deaf child.
Parents often look for cures, hope against hope their child's hearing will get better, or cling to the idea that their deaf child will grow
into a hearing adult.

Our aim in this chapter is to provide the basic information to
help you understand the way the ear works, what can go wrong,
the different tests which are used and how they work, and finally
to look briefly at some of the main causes of deafness. The more
you know about your child's hearing loss the more you will be able
to tackle the challenge which faces you.

How the Ear Works

In Figure 1.1 the structure of the ear together with the names
of various parts of the hearing system are shown. To avoid confusion, laymen's terms are generally used but the medical terms are
included for reference. Sounds enter the ear canal (1) *(external
auditory meatus)*, and are funnelled down to meet the eardrum (2)
(tympanic membrane). As sounds hit the eardrum they make it
vibrate; the type of sound will vary the rate of vibration, low tones
causing a slower rate of vibration than high tones. Attached to the
back of the eardrum is a bone known as the hammer (3) *(malleus)*.
This bone is one of three tiny bones which are connected together
and form a flexible bridge across the middle ear. Any movement
of the eardrum will move the hammer which will cause the anvil
(4) *(incus)* to move the stirrup (5) *(stapes)*. These three small
bones are sometimes referred to as the *ossicular chain*. They have
two purposes: one is to transmit vibrations of sounds from the
outer ear to the inner ear, the other is to amplify the level of that
sound to give the inner ear the clearest possible message. The middle ear is normally filled with air but the inner ear is filled with
fluid. There is an increase in loudness of sounds as they move
across the bones of the middle ear; this helps to make the trans-

mission of the sound from air to liquid more effective. The outer and middle ear are a mechanical system, and any breakdown in this part of the hearing mechanism can usually be medically or surgically treated.

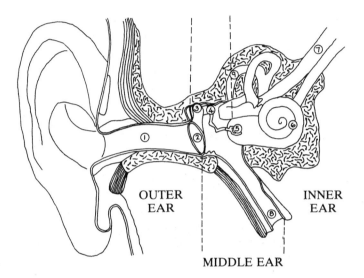

OUTER EAR

INNER EAR

MIDDLE EAR

(1) Ear Canal *(external auditory meatus)*
(2) Eardrum *(typanic membrane)*
(3) Hammer Bone *(malleus)*
(4) Anvil Bone *(incus)*
(5) Stirrup *(stapes)*
(6) Cochlea
(7) Auditory Nerve
(8) Eustachian Tube
(9) Semicircular Canals

FIGURE 1.1 *Structure of the human ear*

Beyond the stirrup is the inner ear. The stirrup bone is attached to a small flexible membrane called the oval window; this is situated on the cochlea (6), a boney structure shaped like a snail shell. The cochlea is divided into two chambers and is filled with fluid. The membrane which divides the cochlea into two parts has thousands of hair-like cells along it. As the stirrup rocks to and fro into the oval window waves are formed in the fluid of the cochlea. The waves move along the membrane and move the hair cells. There are approximately 17,000 of these hair cells and when any one of these is stimulated enough they send electrical messages to the connecting nerve. These messages are passed along the auditory nerve (7) to the brain. The nerve system works like a telephone wire; it transmits electrical impulses, the messages from the hair cells in the cochlea, to the parts of the brain which specialise in decoding information about sounds. The brain uses this information in the same way as a computer would, to make sense of the information it receives and to understand the message. Figures 1.2 and 1.3 give a representation of how sounds pass from the outer ear to the listening centres of the brain.

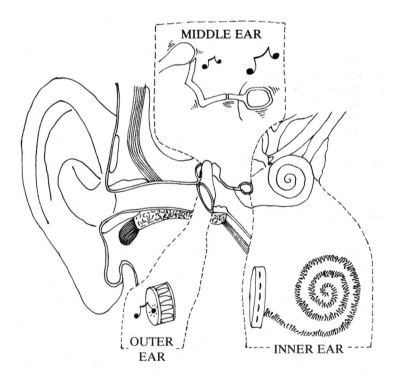

FIGURE 1.2 *The passage of sound in the human ear*

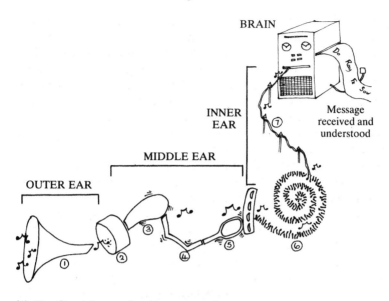

(1) Ear Canal *(external auditory meatus)*
(2) Eardrum *(typanic membrane)*
(3) Hammer Bone *(malleus)*
(4) Anvil Bone *(incus)*
(5) Stirrup *(stapes)*
(6) Cochlea
(7) Auditory Nerve

FIGURE 1.3 *Sound going through the hearing system in a 'normal' ear*

Why Can't My Child Hear?

Figure 1.4 gives a simplified picture of problems affecting the hearing system.

OUTER EAR

At the simplest level, wax in the ear canal can cause a mild hearing loss. Wax can be softened with drops — sodium bicarbonate drops or olive oil are recommended — and then syringed out if necessary. The presence of wax is quite normal. It helps to protect the eardrum from dirt and germs. Occasionally children

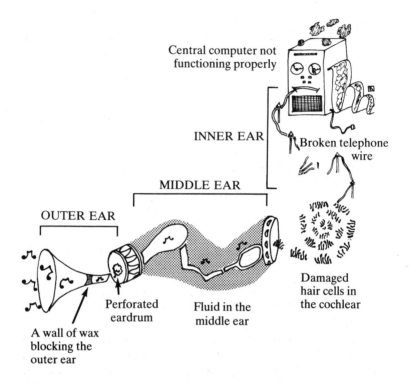

Central computer not
functioning properly

INNER EAR

Broken telephone
wire

MIDDLE EAR

OUTER EAR

Perforated
eardrum

Fluid in the
middle ear

Damaged
hair cells in
the cochlear

A wall of wax
blocking the
outer ear

FIGURE 1.4 *Some problems which may affect the hearing system*

have small growths in their ears which require medical treatment.
The skin which lines the ear canal can be affected by eczema; this
does not normally affect hearing but can cause problems in making
use of a hearing aid.

MIDDLE EAR

In the UK one in four children under the age of seven have a
hearing loss at some time because their middle ear is not functioning normally. The most common problem is fluid in the middle
ear; the three bones, rather than moving in air-filled space, have
to move through liquid. Imagine walking briskly down the road
and then walking at the same speed in a swimming pool — you
would find it impossible. In just the same way fluid in the middle

ear makes any movement of the bones harder. Noises have to be louder to get the bones vibrating at a level where the sound would be passed on to the inner ear. Loud sounds can by-pass the middle ear; they are transmitted through the bones of the skull and directly stimulate the cochlea.

Normally the middle ear is kept ventilated by a tube which runs from the middle ear to the back of the throat. This is the Eustachian tube (8) (see Figure 1.1). People are usually able to open their Eustachian tubes simply by swallowing. This is useful to relieve the feeling of 'full ears' when going up a steep hill or when taking off in an aeroplane. If this tube becomes blocked by swelling as a result of a cold, or by pressure exerted by swollen adenoids, the middle ear cannot be ventilated. Fluid develops within the middle ear space and thickens to the consistency of glue — hence the term 'glue-ear', medically known as *serous otitis media*. If this condition persists it may be necessary to take surgical action. A minor operation called a myringotomy is performed. A tiny hole is made in the eardrum to allow the fluid to be sucked out. A small plastic tube or grommet may be put in the eardrum, one end in the outer ear and the other in the middle ear. This helps to keep the middle ear ventilated. The eardrum heals naturally and in healing it pushes the tube out. The amount of time this takes varies enormously. This procedure may need to be carried out more than once, but repeated insertion of grommets will scar the eardrum.

Earache is usually caused by an infection entering the middle ear via the Eustachian tube or through a hole (perforation) in the eardrum. The infection will cause pus to be formed; as this builds up in the middle ear it presses against the eardrum causing pain. This condition is known as *acute otitis media*. Medical treatment is necessary as untreated infections cause damage to the bones of the middle ear. In severe cases, where there have been numerous infections, the mastoid bone situated behind the ear may be infected or the ossicular chain in the middle ear destroyed. Fortunately both of these conditions are less likely to occur as a child gets older. In young children the Eustachian tubes are nearly horizontal, making it hard for them to drain naturally. As a child gets older and his facial bone structure develops, the Eustachian tubes become more vertical, allowing easy drainage of the middle ear.

Hearing loss caused by problems affecting the outer or middle ear is known as *conductive loss*. Any child, whether or not they have a nerve deafness (see below), can have a conductive hearing loss. These losses usually respond to medical treatment. Any child with a conductive loss should be referred for medical advice to ensure that the cause is treated and the effects kept to a minimum. Remember to ask what the tests have shown and why your child requires treatment. Often parents misunderstand, as one parent noted: 'I had no idea what grommets were or why he needed them, perhaps the doctor thought I knew because I am deaf.'

INNER EAR

Any damage to the inner ear, the cochlea, the nerve pathways or the part of the brain which deals with sound, is permanent. This type of loss is known as sensori-neural, perceptive or nerve deafness. The different names can be a source of confusion and of misplaced hope. Damage to any part of the inner ear cannot be treated medically or surgically. This is a very hard thing for any parent to accept; naturally one wants to try anything which might help, perhaps seek miracle cures or second, third or even fourth opinions. One mother described her search for a cure for her daughter's deafness:

> We tried everything we had heard about deafness. We travelled to Austria and Paris to see specialists, we had to try everything, we thought at first there was a chance to cure her deafness. As we listened and learnt more we began to slowly accept that we were grabbing at straws. My daughter is profoundly deaf, she needs the best hearing aids and our love and understanding.

A grandmother was frustrated and annoyed by friends' inability to accept her grandchild's deafness: 'It is so irritating when people ask you if your grandchild's hearing is "getting better" as if it's an illness.'

A further difference between conductive and sensori-neural losses is that in a conductive loss, only loudness is affected, whereas in a sensori-neural loss the *quality* of sounds is affected as well. However loud sounds are made, a child with a sensori-neural loss will only hear a distorted pattern of sound. Some sounds may never be heard at all. There is an added difficulty that children with sensori-neural losses may face: this is an inability to tolerate loud sounds. In these cases sounds need to be amplified in order to be heard but as the sound level builds up it becomes uncomfortable, even painful. This is known as *recruitment*. The type of hearing aids that are fitted is of crucial importance if a person with recruitment problems is to be able to make use of their aids.

Tinnitus is a condition where noises are heard that are not being produced in the environment. These noises are often likened to roaring or buzzing, to whistling kettles, bells and banging. There is a considerable amount of research in this area. Tinnitus is fairly common in the adult hearing impaired population; little is reported about children with tinnitus, which may merely reflect a lack of research in this area. If a child has always experienced tinnitus he will consider it to be normal and an understanding of the situation will only come later when someone explains that this is not the case.

In a sensori-neural hearing loss one usually finds that high frequency sounds are most affected. The tiny hair cells in the cochlea respond to particular frequencies; those nearest the oval window are responsible for relaying high frequency sounds. These cells are most open to damage because they are nearest to the oval window. Whilst hearing aids will make sounds louder they cannot help a child to hear sounds which his ear is unable to perceive. The high frequency sounds are often badly distorted or may be missing altogether in severe cases. Yet high frequency sounds are very important because they carry a lot of information, as this example shows:

_a_e a _i_e _a_

Here is a familiar phrase with all the consonants removed. The consonants are typically high frequency sounds. If you can understand the message — congratulations, you have exceptionally good decoding skills! If we take the same phrase and remove the vowels but add the consonants you should find the message easier to understand:

H_v_ _ n_c_ d_y

The message is simply 'Have a nice day'. A listener, given vowels alone, faces a much harder task in understanding a message than a listener given consonant clues. Clearly a severe sensori-neural loss is going to present a considerable problem to anyone, but particularly to a small child starting to develop speech.

Hearing Tests: What is Measured?

> I remember being told Beth had lots of useful hearing: what is useful hearing — did they mean she wasn't really deaf? I simply had nothing to measure it against.

It is not enough to know simply that a child has a hearing loss. We need to know which sounds are affected and to what degree. Once this information is available help can be offered, varying from medical treatment to the fitting of hearing aids. Hearing is tested across a range of sounds from low tones to high tones. Hearing tests usually use five frequencies, 250 Hertz, 500 Hertz, 1000 Hertz, 2000 Hertz and 4000 Hertz. Hertz (Hz) is simply the term used to describe the number of cycles per second in any tone; for example, a tone of 250 Hz would complete 250 cycles per second, while tones of a higher frequency would complete more cycles per second, 4000 Hz completing 4000 cycles. As a rough guide middle C on a piano is about 256 Hz. Hearing tests use these frequencies because they are the ones which are most important for understanding human speech. As the frequency range becomes reduced the quality of speech begins to be lost as sounds become distorted. Some examples of high, middle and low frequency sounds are given in Figure 1.5.

Low frequency	Middle frequency	High frequency
a as in hat *oo* as in food *ow* as in tow	*ay* as in play *ee* as in see *d* as in dog	*s* as in sun *f* as in face *h* as in horse *th* as in thin
frequency spread 25–500 Hz	500–2000 Hz	2000–8000 Hz

FIGURE 1.5 *Examples of speech sounds of various frequencies*

The telephone system in the UK uses a range of sounds from 300 to 3300 Hz. The low frequency vowels are easy to hear, but what of the consonants? Many consonants are not transmitted or are severely distorted, which is why it is often hard to make sense of names of unfamiliar words on the telephone and why people are often asked to spell things out to avoid confusion.

In addition to knowing which sounds can be heard it is important to establish how loud the sound has to be in order for the child to hear it. The loudness of any particular frequency is measured in decibels (dB). One mother's comments clearly underline the sort of problem parents face in making sense of test information which has been offered to them: 'I was told my son had an average loss of 90dB but I don't understand what that means. Does it mean he can hear 90% of what is going on or 10%? Is it good or bad? I just don't know.' It is very important to understand that the decibel scale is not a simple scale like that on a thermometer, where a change from 36°C to 37°C is the same difference as a change from 38°C to 39°C. The decibel scale used runs from −20dB to 140dB, but each increase in 10dB is actually increasing the sound by the power of 10. This is illustrated in Figure 1.6.

0		
10	10	
20	10 × 10	20db is 10 times louder than 10dB
30	10 × 10 × 10	
40	10 × 10 × 10 × 10	
decibels 50	10 × 10 × 10 × 10 × 10	
(db) 60	10 × 10 × 10 × 10 × 10 × 10	
70	10 × 10 × 10 × 10 × 10 × 10 × 10	

thus 70dB is 1,000,000 times louder than 10dB (i.e. 1 million times louder)

FIGURE 1.6 *The decibel scale: a scale to the power of 10*

Clearly, using the decibel scale keeps the numbers manageable but it is easy to forget that the difference between a 50dB loss and a 70dB loss is vast. It is perhaps easier to understand the decibel scale if sound levels are related to everyday experiences; Figure 1.7 gives some simple examples.

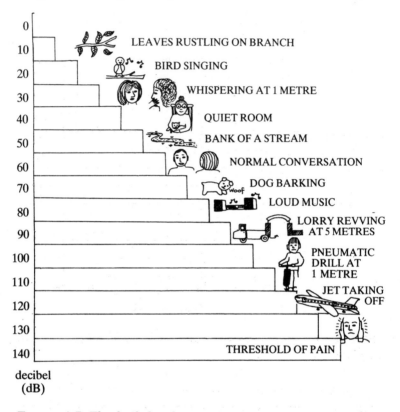

decibel (dB)
0
10   LEAVES RUSTLING ON BRANCH
20   BIRD SINGING
30   WHISPERING AT 1 METRE
40   QUIET ROOM
50   BANK OF A STREAM
60   NORMAL CONVERSATION
70   DOG BARKING
80   LOUD MUSIC
90   LORRY REVVING AT 5 METRES
100 PNEUMATIC DRILL AT 1 METRE
110
120 JET TAKING OFF
130
140 THRESHOLD OF PAIN

FIGURE 1.7 *The decibel scale*

AUDIOGRAMS

As a hearing test is carried out, the sound level at which each test frequency is first heard is plotted on a graph called an *audiogram*. Frequency is plotted from left to right and hearing loss in dB from top to bottom (see Figure 1.8). Threshold levels at each frequency are plotted separately for each ear. The symbol for the right ear using headphones is 0, and for the left ear is X. If there is no response it is recorded as NR. The shaded area represents an area known as the speech curve; this is the area which normal speech characteristically falls within. If hearing levels fall below the speech curve on the audiogram some components of normal speech will be misheard or lost altogether.

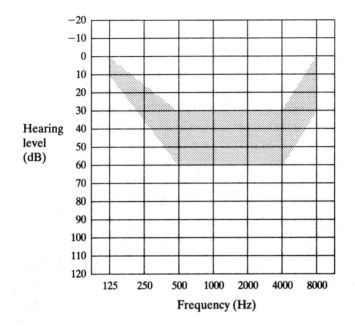

FIGURE 1.8 *A pure tone audiogram graph on which the audiogram is plotted*

A number of audiograms are now shown, illustrating varying degrees of hearing loss. Figure 1.9 shows that the patient has hearing within normal limits: any variation between 0 and 25dB is accepted as normal hearing. The audiogram in Figure 1.10 illustrates a mild hearing loss in both ears; this type of 'flat' loss is typical of a conductive hearing loss. Sounds will be muffled and unclear. Conductive losses vary considerably from day to day, so that a child may hear little of what is being said on one day but hear normally the next. Conductive losses tend to recur and children can become confused and insecure as a result of this. It appears to them that on some days everyone is including them and talking normally, and on other days everyone is whispering and excluding them. The child may hear what is said directly to him but may miss out on the general chat at home or in the classroom. Some children

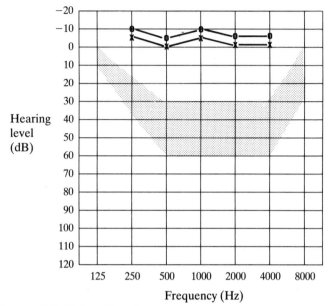

FIGURE 1.9 *Normal hearing*

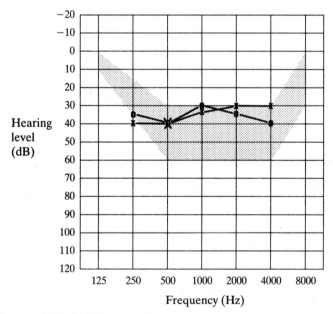

FIGURE 1.10 *Mild hearing loss*

are more directly affected and may b⌐ slow to develop speech, or have very unclear speech. A girl who had suffered from a conductive hearing loss throughout her school career made the following comments:

> The thing which really gets on my nerves most is when a teacher says something and I don't hear them. If I say 'pardon' they often say I should have been listening. I am all behind at school. It's no fun if you can't hear half of what people are saying and you keep getting things wrong. Everyone just thinks you're thick.

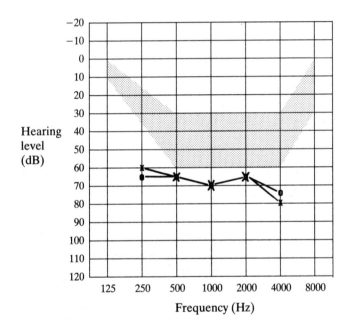

FIGURE 1.11 *A severe hearing loss affecting both ears*

Figure 1.11 shows a more significant loss; the sounds have to be raised to an average of 68dB before the patient responds. The hearing falls completely outside the speech area. A child born with this degree of hearing loss would hear very little of normal conversational speech; a hearing aid would be needed to make the sounds loud enough for the child to hear. The child would be aware of loud environmental sounds such as a lorry driving past, or a door slamming. Parents could easily confuse these responses with being able to hear normally, and it may only become obvious that a child is in difficulty if he fails to develop normal speech and language. It would be very difficult for a child born with this degree of loss to develop speech normally without some special help — this is discussed in following chapters.

Figure 1.12 shows that whilst hearing in the low frequencies is normal the mid and high frequencies show a severe loss. Without a hearing aid, a child with this loss would gain a lot of vowel information but miss out most of the consonants. The vowels are not only low frequency, they are also louder than the consonants. In their early years children with this type of loss sometimes fail to be diagnosed because they use their normal hearing in the low frequencies to respond to their name, the door banging, or people giving simple instructions. They will start to talk but soon it will become more obvious that there is a problem as certain speech sounds are missed and mistakes become more noticeable. It can be very problematic trying to provide suitable hearing aids for the pattern of hearing revealed in this type of audiogram.

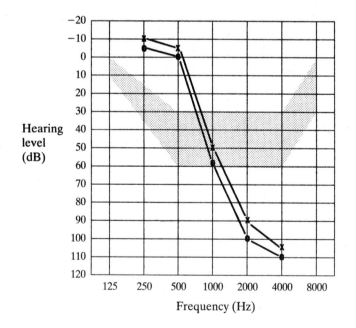

FIGURE 1.12 *A high frequency loss*

The audiogram in Figure 1.13 shows a profound hearing loss across the speech frequencies. This is often referred to by audiologists as a 'bottom corner' audiogram with a profound loss in the low and mid frequencies and little or no measurable hearing in the high frequencies. Children with this type of loss will not hear anything of normal speech. Even with the help of powerful hearing aids they will only hear a very distorted pattern of speech and will need to use both vision and hearing to understand speech. Early specialised help is of critical importance. Children with this type of hearing loss are the ones who may have most to gain from the use of sign input. These children will, of necessity, rely heavily on their vision to help them communicate.

In addition to hearing being tested via headphones, to find the air conduction thresholds, it is also possible to test ability to hear sounds conducted through the bones of the skull. The procedure is the same as for air conduction but this time the child wears a small vibrator which is usually placed on the mastoid bone behind the ear. When testing through headphones (air conduction), the whole hearing system, outer, middle and inner ear, is

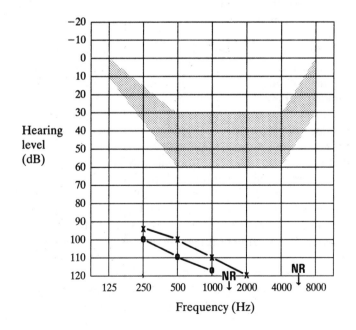

FIGURE 1.13 *A profound hearing loss*

being tested; testing using a vibrator (bone conduction), allows
the audiologist to exclude the outer and middle ear and test the
inner ear alone. In this way the audiologist can separate the hearing loss into conductive and sensori-neural hearing loss. To sum-
marise this information:

Air conduction = outer + middle + inner ear
                 └──────┬──────┘ └────┬────┘
                     conductive   sensori-neural

Bone conduction = inner ear = part of hearing loss which can-
                  └────┬────┘   not be improved medically
                   sensori-neural

An example is given to illustrate this; two children were
tested using headphones and produced very similar audiograms
(Figure 1.14). Bone conduction testing was then completed and
this information added to the audiograms, symbolised by △
(Figure 1.15).

In the case of audiogram (i) the bone conduction responses
are normal and the air conduction responses are down; the results
show that the inner ear is working normally but either the outer or
the middle ear is not functioning properly. This child has a conductive hearing loss which can be treated. The situation in audiogram
(ii) is quite different: responses for both air and bone conduction
are down below normal limits. When the inner ear alone was
tested by bone conduction the result was not improved. In this
case the loss is sensori-neural, and medical or surgical help will
be of no benefit. The fact that a child has a sensori-neural loss
does not exclude him from having a conductive loss as well. In this
case the situation is called a *mixed loss*. Any conductive element
overlaying a sensori-neural loss should receive prompt medical
attention.

Many parents will have heard of cochlear implants and
believe that an implant will restore normal hearing; certainly,
cochlear implants are an aid to hearing but they do not offer the
chance to hear normally. (This area is discussed more fully in
Chapter 3.)

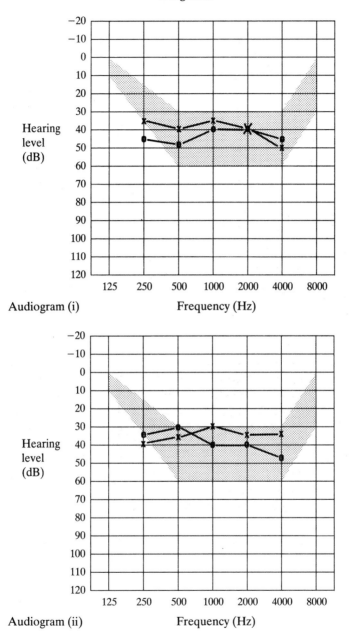

Audiogram (i)

FIGURE 1.14 *Audiograms of two children tested using headphones (air conduction)*

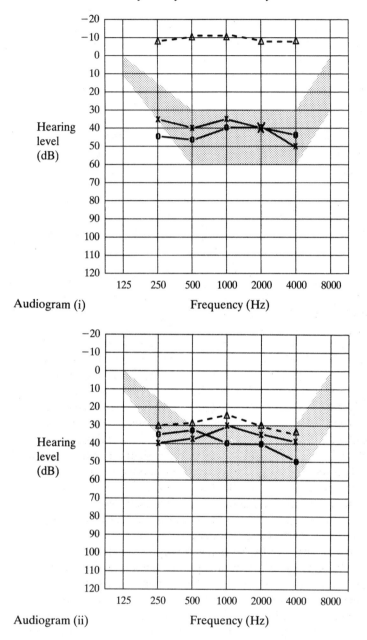

Audiogram (i)

Audiogram (ii)

FIGURE 1.15 *Audiograms of two children tested via both air and bone conduction*

It is common for parents to compare audiograms. Parents start to worry if their child is doing less well than another child with a similar audiogram. It is all too easy to get depressed and feel that you are getting it wrong, whereas in reality the other child may have less distortion, less recruitment, less tinnitus. That child can therefore be expected to do better regardless of the efforts of all concerned. (Father of profoundly deaf son.)

IMPEDANCE TESTING

Impedance testing is a routine part of any hearing assessment. It is simple and quick to carry out and can be used with very young children as the only requirement is that they sit still momentarily. A small probe is inserted into the ear canal. The probe contains three channels: one feeds a low frequency tone into the ear canal, the second measures the pressure in the ear canal and the third measures the amount of sound which is reflected back by the eardrum. In a normal healthy ear the pressure on both sides of the eardrum is equal, which allows the eardrum to vibrate freely and pass on sounds via the three bones to the inner ear. Part of the sound which hits the eardrum bounces back off it into the ear canal. If the pressure on each side of the eardrum is not equal the eardrum becomes stiff and this makes it very difficult for sound to be passed on to the inner ear (conducted) or bounced back into the ear canal (reflected). Impedance measurements test the workings of the eardrum, the bones of the middle ear, the *ossicular chain* and the small muscles attached to the ossicular chain. These muscles protect the inner ear from excessive noise by contracting and stiffening the ossicular chain when noise reaches levels between 70dB and 90dB (see Figure 1.7). This muscle activity is called the *stapedial reflex*. The audiologist will use the information gained from the impedance tests together with other test information to form a clear idea of what is happening in the child's hearing system. Impedance information is plotted out automatically on a *tympanogram*. Both the shape of the tympanogram and the point at which the eardrum shows a maximum ability to move, *compliance*, are considered. Figure 1.16 illustrates some tympanogram patterns and the types of problem that can be associated with them.

Whilst impedance testing can be performed on very young children, pure tone testing to produce an audiogram presents

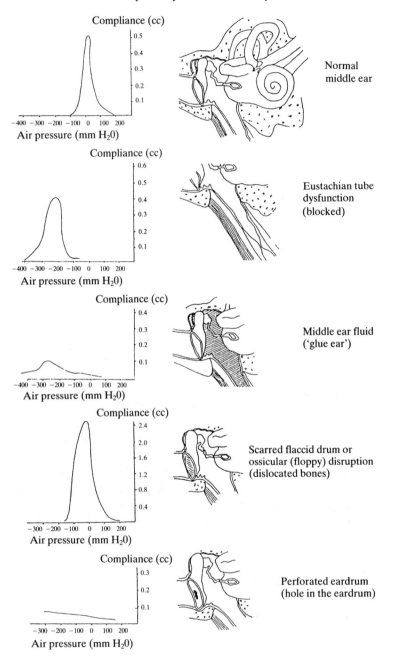

FIGURE 1.16 *Tympanogram shapes and associated problems*

more of a problem. Children under the age of about two years will not be able to complete standard pure tone audiometry. Two different types of tests can be used with these children. One looks at the child's responses to sounds, normally a turning response towards the source of the sound; sounds of different frequencies are used and the level of sound is mechanically measured so that responses can be related to a pure tone audiogram. The second type of test does not require the child to be directly involved, and so can be used on very young children or children who are unable to be tested by standard methods because of other difficulties. This second type of test is being increasingly used but tends to be centred in large hospitals. They are grouped together under the name of Evoked Response Audiometry (ERA).

EVOKED RESPONSE AUDIOMETRY

Evoked response audiometry tests the nerve pathways of hearing. These tests are based on the fact that when the hearing system responds to sound, the auditory nerve is activated; this activity produces an electrical change in the nerve. These changes are minute but by the use of sophisticated equipment they can be measured. In all the tests electrodes are attached to the subject's head; these allow electrical activity in the brain to be picked up. Sounds are presented a number of times, which allows a small computer to pick up the particular brain activity which is a response to sound. When the sound becomes too quiet for the subject to hear, the nerves are not activated and there is no response. ERA is a starting point; from the test results the audiologist can start to get other professionals involved. Hearing aids can be issued, but with caution. The limited information that is available to the audiologist means that she will be constantly seeking further information about the child's response to his hearing aids. As it becomes possible to use other tests, hearing aids can be modified appropriately. It is sad to note that the common mistake of many parents is to misunderstand the limited amount of information that ERA tests give. These tests are excellent pointers, but they are only a starting point. Figure 1.17 summarises some basic information on four ERA tests, of which the most commonly used is the Brainstem Auditory Evoked Response (BSER).

Do not be afraid to ask exactly what any test has shown, exactly what information has been obtained and specifically what it means in relation to your child. The professionals are there to offer you their expertise, so make use of it.

Parents in a highly anxious and emotional state are often unable to take in the information they are offered. All too often, in our experience, lack of response to Brainstem Evoked Response testing (2000–3000 Hz area) is taken to mean that their child has no hearing at all; in fact, as there is no low frequency information, the exact hearing loss of any child will only become apparent in time.

Brainstem Auditory Evoked Response (BSER)	This test gives hearing levels within 10dB of thresholds. The major problem is that it only measures hearing in the high frequencies, usually 2000–3000 Hz.
Electro Cochleography (ECochG)	The major difficulty is that this test must be carried out under general anaesthetic and is similar to minor surgery. Test frequencies are widespread; the test does not give low frequency information.
Post Auricular Myogenic Response (PAM)	This test is not reliable as a diagnostic test. Lack of response can occur, even with normal hearing. The test has to use loud noises, 60dB or 80dB, and could easily miss a high frequency loss.
Slow Vertex Response or Cortical Electrical Response (CER)	This is the only ERA test which looks at specific frequencies. It is not suitable for use with small children as test results are affected by movement, attention and sedation.

FIGURE 1.17 *ERA tests*

Your Child is Deaf — But Why?

CAUSES OF DEAFNESS

When anything is found to be wrong, to be different, anyone's natural reaction is to look for a cause. When parents suddenly find their child is different it is quite usual for them to try to find out why. They want to regain control, to see what can be done to help, to explain to family and friends. Most of all parents want to know what has happened to their child and why it has happened. It is important to state at this point that in up to 60% of all cases of hearing impairment the cause of deafness is unknown. Causes of hearing loss can be broadly divided into those present at birth (Congenital); those acquired after birth (Acquired); and Unidentified. Our intention is not to attempt a medical discussion of causes of deafness but to give a brief outline of the main causes. Anyone requiring more detailed information should discuss their case fully with the Ear, Nose and Throat consultant who is involved. Further information is available from a number of texts; we recommend particularly R. D. Freeman, C. F. Carbin and R. J. Boese (1981), *Can't Your Child Hear?*; and B. McCormick (1988), *Screening for Hearing Impairment in Young Children*.

Congenital (present at birth)

Genetic conditions (family history of deafness)

Maternal rubella (German measles during pregnancy)

Prematurity

Ototoxic drugs taken by the mother during pregnancy (these may successfully treat the mother but damage her unborn baby's hearing)

Cytomeglavirus (virus affecting the unborn child)

Rhesus incompatibility (where mother and baby have different blood groups; if untreated, problems at birth can cause difficulties).

It should be noted that genetic conditions can be divided into three different types: (a) dominant, (b) recessive and (c) sex-linked. Children inherit genes from each parent. In the case of a dominant condition only one parent needs to carry the gene responsible for deafness; there is a one in two chance of the children being affected. In the case of recessive deafness both parents hear normally; at conception a recessive gene carrying the deafness from one parent meets the matching recessive gene from the other parent, and in this case the baby will be born with a hearing loss. There is a one in four chance of children being affected in this way. Where the cause of deafness is sex-linked it is an abnormality within the chromosomes which results in deafness. This is a complex area dealt with in detail in *Can't Your Child Hear?* by Freeman, Carbin and Boese. Parents needing advice should be encouraged to seek genetic counselling from a specialist.

Acquired deafness
The most common causes of hearing loss acquried in childhood are:
   Meningitis
   Head trauma (severe accident to the head)
   Ototoxic drugs (certain drugs used to treat severe illness may
      have the side effect of causing deafness)
   Mumps $\Big\}$ Frequently result in a severe hearing loss in one ear
   Measles
   Conductive hearing loss.

Unidentified
In 30 to 60% of all cases of sensori-neural deafness no cause can be pinpointed. It is often hard for parents to accept that it is not possible to identify a cause of their child's handicap. The really important thing is to seek specialist advice. If no known cause can be found for the hearing loss, it can be hard for parents to accept; but although you cannot change what has happened, you can greatly affect how your child will grow and develop. There is a lot to learn about. Will a hearing aid help? What other specialised equipment is available? Who is there to advise and support you? The most important thing to remember is summed up by a mother of a deaf child:

> . . . that Carrie would never hear music, the wind howling but most of all she would never hear us say how much we loved her; oh how foolish we were, she has given us so much love and laughter. She is a child who is deaf, not a deaf child.

CHAPTER 2
Family Reactions

There is no correct or incorrect reaction to being told that your child has a permanent hearing loss. There is a flood of emotion which must neither be dammed up nor allowed to sweep you away. No one can predict how any particular family will react; this depends on many factors. As a deaf adult Hilary was in the position of understanding what deafness meant; to her it was the norm, yet this did not mean that the formal diagnosis of her son as being profoundly deaf was a completely worry-free period:

> They decided to do brainstem on him at the hospital. After the test I was told he had no response at all; this upset me greatly. Deep down I knew he was deaf but to be stone deaf was extremely rare. I was completely taken aback . . . The peripatetic teacher came round that evening to talk about hearing aids and my first reaction was immediately 'no'. I couldn't see that putting a hearing aid on a four-month-old baby would help, especially when I was told he had no response. To say I was a bit upset was an understatement. It was Fiona's playgroup leader who had the most helpful advice. She said, 'Never mind, you are the best person to help him, having gone through the experience yourself.' Everyone else had said they were sorry but I knew then she was right, it was up to me to help him as best as I could.

As a teacher of the deaf Wendy has faced the other end of the problem.

> Parents are upset, devastated and often aggressive; this is to be expected. They are full of questions which are impossible

Common reactions to diagnosis of hearing loss

to answer. When will our child learn to speak? What sort of
school will he go to? and so on. They are in a very vulnerable
position. It is important for them to see you in a positive light
but not as the 'source of all knowledge about deafness', no
one is that. Some parents want to rush into action and try anything and everything straight away, others are numb and
unable to take anything in at all. Families need time, support
and advice so they can make informed decisions about their
child. They do not need pushing, converting to a particular
approach or to be 'carried around' by professionals who are
keen to be invaluable.

To the majority of parents deafness is something they know
little about. When they are told their child is deaf they are faced
with a totally unknown quantity. The child whom they know
better than any other person is suddenly labelled with something
which is completely foreign to them. The hearing test can be
worrying to parents, and a negative result is often devastating:

Brainstem — I remember thinking it sounded awful, what on earth were they going to do to her? They explained she'd have to be put to sleep and have things stuck on her head — I couldn't cope at all. My husband took the day off to go to the hospital. There were a lot of children being tested and they were all fine, no problems. We were last. They came out and said she was profoundly deaf — I didn't hear those words. I was so shocked, I just felt ignorant. I said 'oh you mean she'll have to wear deaf aids?' 'No', they said, 'hearing aids.' I felt so stupid, I didn't know anything about deafness. It was all arranged, we were given an appointment the next day, a bus route, times and so on. It was all too much. I felt so awful. They asked me if I'd realised she was deaf, hadn't I banged doors or shouted or anything? I think I would have liked a little time just to let it sink in — to have someone to chat to, not appointments and official people. (Mother of a profoundly deaf girl.)

It is natural for parents to want their children to be happy and healthy, and to live a full life, so diagnosis of a hearing loss is inevitably a shock. Parents no longer know what to expect. Here are a number of extracts from parents' accounts which illustrate painful but normal reactions.

I can remember very clearly the absolute devastation. I thought of the simple deaf person who couldn't talk. I saw other little girls chattering together and thought my daughter will never do that. I didn't think she would ever learn to talk.

I was upset when she was diagnosed because it was something I knew nothing about. (Parents' comments about their severely deaf daughter.)

I spent my time in tears just being sad for what was lost and for not understanding Sofie's problem sooner. (Mother of a deafened child.)

When I found out my child was deaf, I cried. I couldn't believe it. I was angry too but I didn't know who with. Then once I got used to the idea I was angry with everyone who kept saying 'no he can't be'. (A deaf mother of a deaf son.)

I just felt grief, I couldn't believe it was true. I spent hours walking around the house with earplugs in trying to imagine what life would be like for him. (Grandmother of a partially hearing child.)

It was a strange time; three or four weeks before we'd had a little boy, now we had an officially deaf child. (Mother of a son who had meningitis.)

Families need to regain control, to balance the situation and to start making some practical adjustments. The whole family is affected by the diagnosis of a specific problem, brothers and sisters, grandparents and neighbours. A sense of panic at not knowing what to do or expect, or of sinking under a mass of advice can easily force parents into a position where they do not know what to do — so they do nothing.

When we were first told Christopher was deaf, I watched my daughter turn from being a happy young wife and mother into a bitter tormented girl. She would not accept that her child was deaf for a long time. When she did at last come to terms with the situation she coped marvellously by expecting Christopher to behave like a hearing child. I have nothing but admiration for my daughter and her husband. (Christopher is partially hearing.)

I felt as if I was the only person in the world who this happened to, the only one who had to struggle to cope. (A mother whose daughter has a dual handicap.)

I tried to be practical and not let it complicate my life, I cried too. A few weeks later all the negative aspects kept coming into my mind. (Mother of a profoundly deaf son.)

It was very important after swimming around in a grey area for so long — we were going to make the decision. We would look at everything, decide what we wanted for our son then put all our energy into it. (Parents of a child deafened by meningitis.)

Parents often feel very isolated, particularly in the early stages. In many cases it is the mother who receives the majority of professional advice and opinion; this puts all the stress of decision making on the mother and in some cases results not only in tension but also in the apportioning of blame:

My husband works away so when Lee was diagnosed as being deaf, I had to tell his parents and they've always blamed me, as if it is my fault. It caused a huge rift which is still there. My husband blames me because I took Lee to be tested!

If you only ever have visits from the teacher of the deaf at times when only one parent can be present because of work, ask if you can arrange to have a chat with all of you together occasionally. Ask if there are evening meetings for parents, contact your local branch of the National Deaf Children's Society, ask to be put in contact with the Social Worker for the Deaf who will be a sympathetic listener, and remember that the peripatetic teacher of the deaf is there to support and advise you too. A list of other contacts is included in Appendix 1.

Sometimes the feeling of isolation is the result of physical isolation, but in other cases the professionals who should be offering support fail in their duties, with unforgiveable results: 'We needed support, information, advice, the chance to talk things over; instead we struggled, we blamed ourselves and we all suffered.' (A family with four children with hearing losses where all were diagnosed very late.)

Through all the emotional turmoil it is easy for parents to become distracted and to forget that whilst their child has a hearing loss, he is in every other way the same child. The special smile he gives you, his favourite toy, splashing in the bath, throwing his half-finished meal across the kitchen, fear of the dog or delight at balloons — none of these reactions will be changed because of a label of deafness. To a child who is born deaf, deafness is accepted, it is what he knows. It can be very difficult for him to understand the looks of worry, sorrow and anger on his parents' faces. He is not aware of what he has done wrong; like all children he simply wants to be accepted.

'We could not accept he was deaf, then someone showed us how he had adapted: if he could see the teacher's face he was fine' (parent of severely deaf son). Children who are deafened face a harder task but show their ability to change and get on with life: 'Justin was the one who adapted, we found it a lot harder' (Justin was deafened by meningitis); 'I don't think she knows she's deaf, she needed time to adjust to her hearing aids but now there are no problems' (parents of a girl deafened at the age of two).

It is easy for any parent to mistake difficult behaviour in a young child as reaction to his hearing loss rather than being normal development. Most two-year-olds have temper tantrums at the most inconvenient times. A determined three-year-old may hold out for what he wants for hours. Sit down strikes, scribbling on the wallpaper, snipping new trousers to see if the scissors work or emptying the contents of the fridge on to the kitchen floor are activities enjoyed by many young children, if not by their parents. Deafness does not cause bad behaviour and it should not be used as an excuse for bad behaviour. The nine-year-old who throws a temper tantrum because he cannot have some sweets, and is excused because he is deaf, is a sad child. The parents have over-compensated for his deafness by allowing him his own way; he manipulates the situation to ensure that he gets what he wants. Life is much harder if you do not know how to behave; people will forgive many things, but rudeness is not one of them. When faced with these situations, as all parents are, simply ask yourself — 'Would I let a hearing child do that?' If the answer is 'No', then it is 'no' for any child. All children make mistakes and learn from them, it helps them to grow. Parents' natural protective role towards their children can be difficult to break but all children have eventually to learn to be independent; the longer you put this off the harder it becomes for all concerned.

> I always feel I want to keep Christopher on a lead even though he is now six, in case he takes off into any danger and I can't reach him in time. (A grandparent's comments.)

> At first we were overprotective, watching her like a hawk, grumbling at her parents for allowing her to play outside, until one day our son-in-law told us we can't cage her in like an animal. She is a normal healthy girl who can't hear. She loves to be with other children and plays very well and other children have accepted her as one of them. (A common reaction felt by grandparents.)

> We know it's important to treat Michael normally, he is almost twenty-two! We do worry, it's like suddenly having a younger child again. I think of all kinds of ridiculous situations, like train crashes and panic, how would he know which way to go if he couldn't hear people shouting. I know it is stupid but I can't help it. (Michael was deafened by meningitis as an adult.)

All children bring their share of joy and laughter, of worry and sadness, and a deaf child is no different. This may seem hard to believe at first but the case studies that are included in the second section of this book may help you to accept this. We hope so.

Brothers and sisters are in a very difficult position. The need to find out about things such as hearing aids and lipreading, as well as attending clinic and the visit of your peripatetic teacher all focus attention away from the rest of the family. Hearing impaired children do have some special needs but in emphasising these, and the major role parents play, it is necessary to stress that *all* family members have their own special needs. It is very easy for brothers and sisters to be excluded, even though this is not done in an intentional way, but creeps in unnoticed. The hearing impaired child needs to be in a position to see to lipread, to be near so he can use his hearing aids, to have things explained clearly and then repeated if necessary. But hearing brothers and sisters need just as much love and reassurance that your time is also available to them, that their strengths and weaknesses are acceptable because they are individuals. The fact that they can hear normally does not mean they will be successful at everything, understand everything or always be understanding and helpful. It is not always easy.

'All the children need support and help and we tried to give all the children an equal amount of attention, as far as we could. We are a family and we do things together and enjoy it. We've all got different limitations.' This mother has three children, one of whom is severely deaf and has spina bifida. Treating any member of the family as special tends only to store up problems which reappear later:

> Angela was handicapped and handicapped people had special status. As far as I was concerned Angela was my sister who happened to be deaf, but my grandfather saw my teasing as taking advantage of her disability. I wasn't allowed to have a normal teasing relationship with my sister. This all seemed very unjust. (Sister of a severely deaf girl.)

Many of the parents we spoke to felt pressured by grandparents, whose reactions varied from complete denial of any problem and refusal to accept the hearing aids, to constant interference and criticism of what was going on. One grandmother's own comment helps to shed light on this sensitive area:

I think the most important thing to remember is that any grandparent is not only worrying about their grandchild, they are also worrying about their child. The more you know the more support you can give, but it is important to support rather than interfere or criticise.

Grandparents' concern for their own children can easily lead them into very similar emotions to those of the parents about their deaf child. All those involved need simply to be a family together, to have time to adjust and think.

Hilary's own words are a thoughtful reminder of the pressures that teachers can unwittingly exert on families:

I really enjoyed Fiona when she was a baby but somehow with Iain I didn't have the time. I always had appointments to go

Acceptance and understanding help to reunite and strengthen family ties

somewhere or someone coming to see me. I was constantly told what I should be doing, nothing could just happen, every little thing had to be planned out. I think I was mentally exhausted when Iain started school.

Many parents are in the position of never having met a deaf person. They associate the word 'deafness' with a highly negative image: the words 'deaf and dumb' always seem to come to mind. Our feeling is that the following comments illustrate the value there is in parents meeting deaf adults and realising that they are as varied as hearing adults. They too may be employed or unemployed, drive a car, get married, own a house, have children and generally get on with life.

I found it hard to believe, then I thought she'd be a deaf child but she'll be able to hear later and just go deaf when she was old — like people often do. Even now, when I know she is profoundly deaf and she will always be, there is a little voice somewhere in my head saying perhaps she will hear again. None of my friends or family believed she was deaf. (Mother of a profoundly deaf child.)

The involvement of an adult deaf person is a good idea, it would help the children to realise that they are always going to be deaf. (Parent of four deaf children.)

A paediatrician's advice to one family was their turning point, after which they were at last able to take decisions after months of helplessness: 'You have a normal little deaf boy here — just go and get on with your lives.' This doctor gave the parents faith in themselves as parents; he reminded them that their little boy was first and foremost a child, and only secondarily did he happen to be deaf. A mother whose son is multiply handicapped in addition to being severely deaf wrote this; her aims are those common to all parents:

He knows he is different but I think he realises his importance, he is there for a reason. The reality is he is deaf in a hearing world so we try to give him every advantage that will make him confident and have some self-esteem. We are not, I think, over-indulgent, we just try our best to make him independent and responsible.

CHAPTER 3
Aids to Hearing

Reactions to Hearing Aids and Daily Routines

Once a child has been diagnosed as having a nerve deafness, parents usually find that they are introduced to hearing aids, and to a teacher of the deaf, and are given plenty to do. Some children with persistent conductive losses are now being fitted with hearing aids. As one mother philosophically noted:

> Leads were often chewed, earmoulds lost, batteries removed but generally the aids were no more trouble than any change in the arrangements would bring from any three-year-old.

Children of any age are individuals who have strong feelings, definite ideas and often seemingly endless determination, so that wearing two small hearing aids can be quite a problem in the early stages. Natural curiosity will mean that the aids are removed and inspected, controls played with, earmoulds chewed and the whole thing hidden in some dark corner of the house — or even the garden:

> We had an awful time with his hearing aids; I dug them up from the potato patch more often than I've dug potatoes.

At the same time that your child is enthusiastically pulling his hearing aids off to get your attention you may well be feeling, quite normally, a mixture of concern, as your teacher of the deaf will encourage you to insist that aids are worn; horror and anxiety, because aids are expensive; fear, in case the aids are hurting; and relief, because they seem so big and cumbersome to you and you would prefer them not to be worn. All this is quite normal. There are very few children who simply let their parents pop their hearing aids on and smile delightedly and proceed without any problems. However, many children soon learn to enjoy their hearing aids and most do not plant them in the garden deliberately. When you buy new shoes they often seem fine in the shop but once you get them home they feel tight, look the wrong shape and are an awful colour. Usually it is not long before the shoes are comfortable and easy to wear. Similarly, when anyone is fitted with hearing aids they feel a little strange. The world will not sound the same, ears will be filled by snugly fitting earmoulds and all this can be a little off-putting. Gradually the aids will simply become part of everyday life, for your child and for you.

If a child is totally resistant to wearing his hearing aids there may be one of several reasons for this. The earmoulds, which should fit snugly into the ear, may be a poor fit and uncomfortable to wear. The hearing aid may be too powerful. The child may be frightened by suddenly hearing sounds which are unfamiliar. One deaf lady recalled being fitted with her first post aural aid:

> It was a very odd sensation, I didn't like it at all. There was a loud rustling noise — awful, and a sharp sound I couldn't understand. It turned out to be the wind and a bird singing.

The other possibility is simply that the child is being totally normal and sees it all as a huge game: 'Mummy and daddy think this is important so if I fuss they will spend lots of time and effort trying to change my mind.' It is like many other things; a determined baby will refuse food which you know is good for him, scream when you take him swimming for fun, refuse to have his teeth cleaned by clamping his mouth shut and remove gloves and hats before you have gone out of the front door. A hearing aid can be one more exciting thing to throw or hide because the reaction from Mum or Dad is dramatic. It is possible to get double-sided stickers or tape or plastic retainer rings — these fit onto behind-the-ear aids and help to keep them in place. Immediately pulling them off becomes less exciting. Gentle but firm encouragement and a willingness to let teddy, dolly or the favourite cuddly toy also try out the hearing aid often helps. If necessary, wait until your child is engrossed in an activity and then gently put the aids on. Beware when young children who normally protest suddenly happily accept their hearing aids. Is it working? Has he switched it off or removed the battery? It is often useful to tape battery compartments closed to prevent exploration of the battery's whereabouts

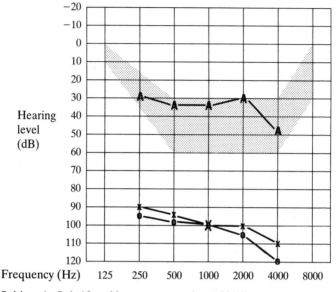

Subject A. S. is 13 and has an average loss of 99dB in the better ear.

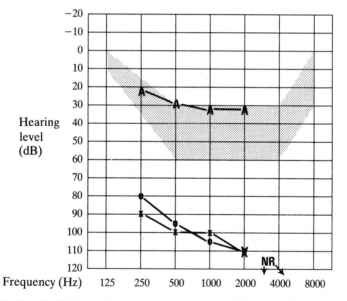

Subject R. W. is 7 and has an average loss of 97dB in the better ear.

FIGURE 3.1 *Aided responses of two profoundly deaf subjects*

and the discovery of how easy it is to remove. Some manufacturers produce battery clips to prevent this.

You may well have mixed feelings about your child wearing hearing aids and society's attitude does not always help. A common thought is 'people who wear glasses are not treated badly, but hearing aids are regarded as a badge of difficulty'. People mistakenly believe that hearing aids correct hearing, that they allow a deaf person to hear normally. This is not the case. Hearing aids are just that, aids to hearing. One deafened eleven-year-old noted:

> They gave me two hearing aids, I didn't like them but it was the only way I could hear. Now I am used to them, I don't think about them at all except when the battery runs out!

Hearing aids are vitally important to almost all hearing impaired children, though there are a few profoundly deaf children who have so little hearing that for practical purposes hearing aids have little to offer. It is impossible for anyone to say exactly which of these children will be able to make some use of their hearing aids; *all* deaf children should, in our opinion, be given the chance of the best hearing aids and encouraged to use them to the best of their ability. Some deaf adults feel very strongly about this because they have bitter memories of being forced to wear aids which were of no practical use to them. Hearing aids are now far more versatile and sophisticated; they are nothing like the aids used fifteen or twenty years ago so the comparison is unfair. For those children who are unable to make use of conventional aids various vibro-tactile aids are available and may be useful.

The two audiograms in Figure 3.1 show the degree of hearing loss together with the aided responses of two children. Both children have profound congenital hearing losses, one averaging 99dB and the other averaging 97dB. The aided response shown is the response to pure tone obtained when listening through hearing aids. In order to simplify the audiograms only the response for the better ear is shown.

When your child has a hearing aid, will he show a definite response to sounds straight away? In a day or two? A week? A month? It is impossible to say and will depend on the degree of hearing loss and the age of the child, amongst other things. Here are a few comments from parents which show these differences. 'He had hearing aids at fourteen months and he loved them, his face lit up, obviously with his aids he could hear'; then from the same mother about another of her children who was also deaf, 'He hated his aids, it was as if they hurt him, he screamed and cried at the sight of them.' This child was later diagnosed as having recruitment (see Chapter 1, page 11). A more common reaction is this:

> When our son first had a hearing aid he went very quiet and withdrawn. I was worried, it didn't seem to help him at all. Then suddenly he was over that and seemed to respond. The teacher of the deaf explained he had been listening to sounds he wasn't used to so he was concentrating. It was all a question of waiting and giving him confidence.

Every parent knows their own child best; here is how one mother approached the problem of getting her partially hearing son to wear his hearing aid.

> It was difficult to explain to a deaf child that he must put something in his ears, but one day he was watching his guinea pig in its cage and it was squeaking, so I hastily popped the hearing aid in his ear and he was thrilled to hear the squeaking. Since then I have no trouble in getting him to wear it and his progress since has been rapid.

One determined mother who had to cope with a well-meaning Grandma who kept taking the aids out to let her grandson 'rest his ears' and neighbours who constantly enquired if 'he really needed those awful aids, poor little mite' was eventually quietly confident. Her feelings were, quite simply, 'I don't care what anyone thinks, he needs his hearing aids in all the time'. We think she is quite right, although there are some notable exceptions.

Hearing aids do not like water so they should not be used in the bath, shower, or swimming pool, and keep your eyes on them during water play at playgroup. Long car journeys can be particularly wearing because the hearing aids will amplify the constant noise of the car engine. A quiet room at home or walking down a noisy street, being in the garden or in an infant classroom — all these situations provide very different noise levels and children, as they get older, will learn to adjust their aids appropriately. Rough and tumble games are great but hearing aids can be damaged or can easily hurt the wearer if bumped. There are deaf children who accept their hearing aids as part of themselves and insist on wearing them in bed. This may seem a little too enthusiastic but the comment of a twelve-year-old profoundly deaf girl gives us a clearer picture:

FIGURE 3.2 *How to break your hearing aid! Try to avoid these situations*

'I wear small post aural aids [behind the ear]. At night I feel a bit frightened without my hearing aids on because it's dark and I can't see very well or hear anything. That feels very lonely.'

Finally, hearing aids are small and easily lost; dogs seem to enjoy chewing them, they break if trodden on, and the last five minutes' scramble to find hearing aids before it is time to leave for school is no fun. These situations can all be avoided if the aids are kept in a box which is put in the same place each evening. It helps if you decorate the box and make it a bit special. Avoid keeping hearing aids on window sills — it makes them very cold to put on in the morning and they will easily get damp. Audiologists and teachers of the deaf know that hearing aids are not childproof and accidents do happen. The most spectacular damage we have seen was when a dog thoroughly chewed a post aural aid and then spat it out in disgust. The poor mother involved was too embarrassed to return it to the hospital herself. In fact it was framed at the hospital and is used to demonstrate that professionals have a sense of humour and, unlike dogs, do not bite!

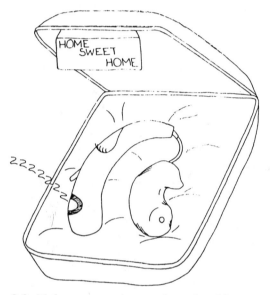

FIGURE 3.3 *Make sure you know where the aids are at the end of each day. Remember to switch them off*

Understanding Hearing Aids

Now that your child has hearing aids what practical things do you need to know? Parents have a key role to play; you cannot expect a baby or small child to look after their own aids so you need to understand at least the basics. You do not have to take a course in micro-electronics but simply take care of the day-to-day handling. For easy reference a separate 'trouble-shooting' section is included at the end of the book, in Appendix 2, which covers:

1. Daily checks
2. When the aid will not work
3. What to do when the aid whistles
4. Care of the earmoulds and plumbing
5. When a radio aid is not working.

In the early stages many parents feel totally bombarded with information which they fear they are not going to remember. But parents very quickly become experts. You will be surprised to find yourself explaining to the milkman, the lady in the shop, grandma and inquisitive friends and neighbours how the aid works, but do it you will.

Parents can listen to everyday sounds through their child's hearing aid by either using a stetoclip (a simple plastic stethoscope which your teacher of the deaf should have), or via their own ear-mould. As well as being a useful check on hearing aid efficiency it provides an insight into hearing aid uses and some problems!

There are various types of hearing aids but they all have the same building blocks — the microphone, the amplifier, the battery, the receiver and the earmould (see Figure 3.4). Sounds enter the hearing aid through the microphone, which acts as a collector of sounds. These sounds are then turned into electrical signals which travel through the amplifier. The amplifier makes the sound louder. The receiver changes the electrical signals back into sounds; from here they travel through the earmould into the ear. The whole system is powered by a battery.

Hearing aids vary in size, shape, weight, colour and performance. There is no one aid to suit all mild hearing losses, nor

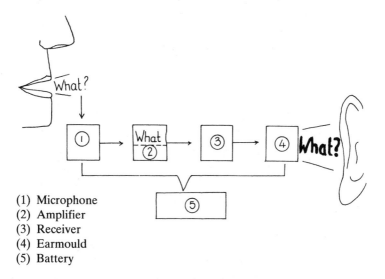

(1) Microphone
(2) Amplifier
(3) Receiver
(4) Earmould
(5) Battery

FIGURE 3.4 *Component parts of a hearing aid*

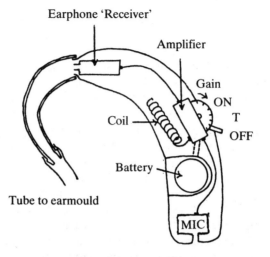

FIGURE 3.5a *Component parts of a behind-the-ear aid (post aural)*

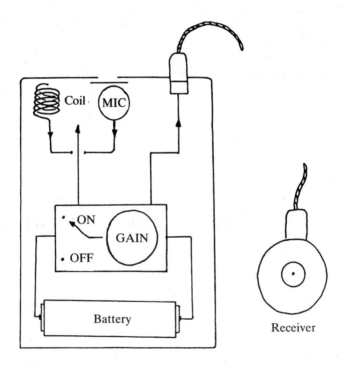

FIGURE 3.5b *Component parts of a body-worn hearing aid*

one for all moderate losses, nor even one for all profound losses. Hearing aids are sophisticated and versatile. Different aids are suitable for different children, even those whose audiograms are apparently similar. There are several different types of aid. *Post aural aids* fit behind the ear; all the parts are housed in the same unit. *Body-worn aids* are larger; they consist of a microphone, battery and amplifier in one unit and the receiver and earmould at ear level. The hearing aid is usually worn on the chest, in a harness or pocket, and a wire attaches it to the receiver and earmould which fits into the ear. *In the ear aids* are aids in which all the working

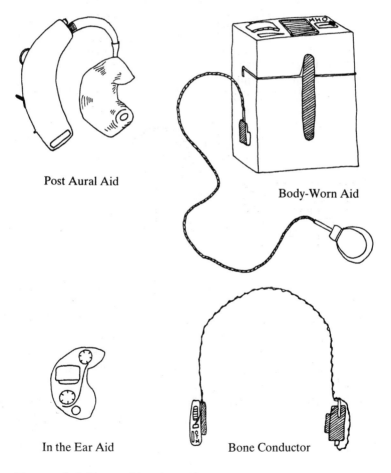

Post Aural Aid

Body-Worn Aid

In the Ear Aid

Bone Conductor

FIGURE 3.6 *Types of hearing aids*

parts are fitted into an earmould and worn in the ear. These aids are not generally felt to be suitable for fitting to children, although technological advances may well mean these will be a real alternative in the near future.

There is a group of children who are unable to wear earmoulds but need to use hearing aids: these are children who either have little or no ear canal or have persistent runny ears as a result of chronic ear infections. In these cases a *bone conductor* is used. The child wears a headband or specially adapted spectacles. The hearing aid or receiver powers a small vibrator which is placed on the mastoid bone behind the ear; the sound travels through the bones of the skull to stimulate the cochlea.

In the UK, the type of hearing aid that any child is prescribed will vary from one part of the country to another. In some areas only post aural aids are issued, in others there is a mix of post aural and body-worn aids. Similarly, the Local Health Authority may issue National Health (NHS) hearing aids or a mixture of NHS and commercial hearing aids. Binaural fitting (an aid for each ear) is generally the norm although some areas may fit only one ear with an aid. As hearing aids are expensive, the choice of aid is often governed by economic factors. In the UK many children are fortunate in being fitted with good quality aids; alas, this is not true of all children.

Body-worn aids are, in theory, more powerful than post aural aids, particularly in amplifying low tones. They are often issued to young profoundly deaf children for this reason. There are some problems in keeping the aid functioning, as children are keen to play and experiment; however, food, play-dough and sand do not improve hearing aid performance! Leads, the wires which run from the hearing aid to the ear, are fun to pull out, chew and tangle round toys. Changing toddlers' clothes and daytime naps are not made easier by having to remove and strap on body-worn aids.

Post aural aids are not as powerful as the body-worn aids. There is also more likely to be a problem of *feedback,* a high-pitched whistle, from the hearing aid; this occurs when the output at the receiver is so loud that it reaches the microphone (Figure 3.7). Feedback distorts the *signal* or message and reduces the amount of amplification. It is more likely to occur when the microphone and receiver are close together, as they are in a post aural aid. In their favour post aural aids provide good localisation, using two ears to decide where a sound comes from. They are less prone

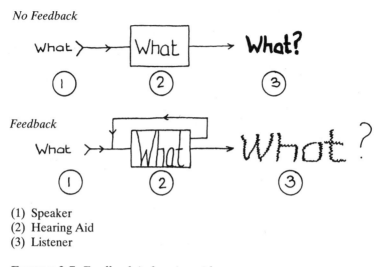

(1) Speaker
(2) Hearing Aid
(3) Listener

FIGURE 3.7 *Feedback in hearing aids*

to the daily wear and tear of an active small child. Clothes will not rub against the aid, giving distortion, as they may with a body-worn aid. It is much more difficult for a small child to fiddle with the controls on post aural aids. However, they are expensive and a lost receiver from a body-worn aid may be easier to replace than a discarded post aural aid. Hearing aids are issued free in the UK and parents should not be expected to insure their child's hearing aids; however, we must emphasise how important it is for parents to check the position about contributions towards payment for damaged or lost aids, although these are only normally a last resort when aids have consistently been wilfully damaged or deliberately lost.

BATTERIES

Hearing aids are powered by batteries; the type of battery used will depend on the type of aid. There are two important things to remember. First, a hearing aid only works efficiently if it has a charged battery in it; just as a dead battery in a car means the car will not move, so a dead battery in a hearing aid means your child cannot hear. Ask your audiologist or teacher of the deaf how often you should change the battery and try to get into a routine. In some cases the children soon let you know if there is a problem:

FIGURE 3.8 *'To think I once drove a mini'*

'She was fitted up with aids and took to them straight away. She was soon able to tell me if the batteries were low or if the aids were not working properly.' In other cases children happily walk around with hearing aids with the battery removed, the aid switched off or a dead battery, so you do have to check the aids regularly.

Post aural aids take small pellet type batteries. There are two types of these small batteries, zinc air and mercuric oxide; check which sort your child's aid uses. Both are easy to swallow, but the mercury batteries are potentially very dangerous to children if swallowed. If this does happen seek medical advice immediately, and stress that the battery is mercuric oxide and known to be dangerous. To avoid this happening you can tape battery compartments closed and simply store spares out of reach in a childproof container. A small plastic shoe called an audio input shoe can be used to ensure that a battery compartment is left unopened. Bathrooms and kitchens are not very good places to store spare batteries as they tend to be steamy places. Do not leave a battery in a hearing aid which is not in use as it may well corrode and leak and so damage the hearing aid. Pellet batteries should be returned to the distribution point for safe disposal.

You do not have to buy batteries; they are supplied free of charge by the National Health Service in the UK. When hearing aids are issued, children are usually given a booklet which enables you to obtain batteries from your local hearing aid centre, hospital, or in some cases, your health centre. The Local Education Service should also ensure that there is a ready supply of batteries available through your teacher of the deaf but it is unreasonable to expect her to carry vast supplies of batteries to cover the needs of all her caseload.

EARMOULDS

'He loved his earmoulds even more than his aids. He spent hours chewing them and more hours having new earmoulds made.' Earmoulds are the part of the hearing aid which are made individually for each user and for each ear. The earmould has to be a good fit in the hearing aid user's ear if the aid is to be used effectively. A variety of materials are in use but there is a general basic procedure in making them. The ear canal is first checked to ensure there is no infection, inflammation or wax in it. Excess wax will probably be removed by syringing to ensure that a good impression of the ear can be taken. A small foam tamp or stopper attached to a piece of cotton is gently inserted into the ear canal; this is to prevent earmould material from going too far down the ear canal. Impression material, which is soft and pliable, is then syringed gently into the ear. It is left there to set, a matter of minutes, then carefully removed. This impression of your child's ear is then used to make an earmould. The earmould can be clear or dyed to suit skin colour and children with sensitive skins can have non-allergic earmoulds. Ask about your child's earmoulds, they are important. Without good earmoulds even the best hearing aid cannot work efficiently. Do not accept an earmould which is a poor fit, even if it is a new mould. Children's ears grow quickly and earmoulds must be regularly replaced to avoid feedback whistle. It is depressing to still hear so many whistling hearing aids in schools. Please go back and ask for new earmoulds to be made. Insist that your child has the best; be sure that your child has as good a listening situation as possible. A word of caution: ear moulds are not the only cause of whistling! A checklist is provided for quick reference (see Appendix 2).

Earmoulds need to be kept clean. It will be easier for everyone if this becomes part of the daily routine, perhaps at bathtime when the hearing aids will have been removed. At first parents will have to clean the earmoulds but do remember that it is important for your child to take on this job, just as they have to take to cleaning their own teeth (see Appendix 2).

RECEIVERS

In the case of a body-worn aid, the receiver clips into the back of the earmould directly. The type of receiver used will be chosen to suit the type of aid, the hearing loss being dealt with, and the size of the child. The type of receiver used does change the response of the hearing aid so not just any receiver will do. Receivers have a code number on them, which should be checked to ensure the aid is being used with the correct receiver. Swopping round at playtime with a best friend, or a rushed change of receiver before assembly or playtime when an aid is faulty, can easily result in the wrong receiver being used. It is now possible to get child-sized receivers for body-worn aids; this is a great help in preventing the weight of the receiver from pulling the earmould out of the child's ear.

CONTROLS

Hearing aids have three basic positions: off, M and T. Normally the 'on' position is M, simply meaning microphone. T is the telecoil position; this position may be used in conjunction with a loop system, or FM induction system (these are discussed in more detail later in this chapter). The volume control on the hearing aid is a numbered dial; you will be advised on the appropriate setting for your child. If a child needs to wear his hearing aid constantly on the maximum, then the aid is not powerful enough and there will be a lot of distortion. Similarly, if an aid needs to be worn on the minimum setting, it is likely to be too powerful and a change of aid may well be indicated.

There are other controls on hearing aids which are set by the audiologist to best suit each child's needs. For example, the shape of a child's hearing loss may well mean he needs more emphasis on the high tones or on the low tones. The audiologist can set this

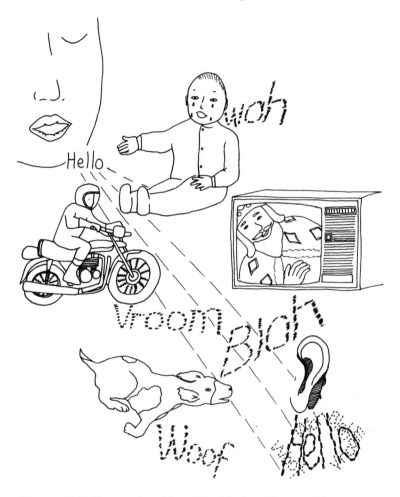

FIGURE 3.9 *Conventional hearing aids amplify everything*

appropriately by altering these controls. Many hearing aids have internal controls which limit the loudness of any sound picked up by the hearing aid. These controls are useful for children who have recruitment — that is, they need sounds amplified but within a short range find the amplification uncomfortable or painful. Special circuits in the hearing aid can limit the maximum output to avoid this situation.

Hearing aids are a vital part of a hearing impaired child's life, but they are only aids and do have their limitations. Hearing aids do not restore 'normal' hearing; they do allow children access to whatever hearing they have and the chance to use this to help them make sense of the world around them. One of the very big drawbacks of conventional hearing aids is that they amplify everything equally. They are not able to pick up speech and at the same time to ignore background noise. This presents considerable problems for children, particularly in partially hearing units and in mainstream schools. A visit to your local school will soon convince you of the high noise levels that can be generated by enthusiastic children. There are various types of hearing aids which can be used to overcome this problem, but inevitably there are some drawbacks to these as well!

Radio Aids

Radio hearing aids consist of two parts: a transmitter, which is worn by the parent or teacher, and a receiver, which is worn by the child. Radio aids overcome the problem of background noise by transmitting the message directly to the child's receiver (see Figure 3.10). This direct link gives the child a clear message and the best chance of understanding in noisy conditions. Radio aids work over a considerable distance, unlike conventional aids which need to be within a metre of the speaker to ensure they amplify efficiently. A radio aid needs to be used appropriately for the child to gain full benefit from it. A teacher who is discussing work with another child should make sure that her transmitter is switched off; similarly a voice suddenly appearing out of nowhere can be disorientating.

Radio aid systems have much to offer the hearing impaired child; the advantages and disadvantages of these compared to conventional hearing aids are summarised in Table 3.1.

Despite the obvious advantages that radio aids have to offer, particularly to children who are integrating into mainstream schools, there is no national policy on provision of radio aids equipment in the UK. There are a variety of methods of funding for radio aid equipment, from the local Education Authorities, the Health Authorities, joint funding from both, and funding from charity and voluntary fund raising. It is hard to understand the hit and miss approach on the provision of radio aid equipment. Education is moving very positively towards integrating the majority

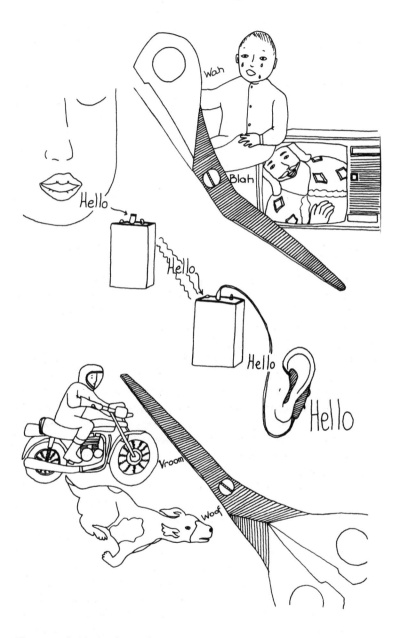

FIGURE 3.10 *Radio aids cut out background noise, providing a direct link from speaker to child*

TABLE 3.1. *Comparison of conventional and radio hearing aids*

Conventional aids	*Radio aids*
1. Free of charge in UK.	Expensive; only some authorities provide them. In other areas families and teachers rely on charity events and fundraising.
2. Small and discreet, lightweight.	Large and more obvious, heavier.
3. Good amplification only close to the source of sound.	Good amplification over considerable distance.
4. Very poor in background noise.	Excellent in background noise.
5. Likely to whistle at high power.	Less likely to whistle than conventional aids (type one radio aids).
6. Good child-to-child link only within restricted area.	Poor child-to-child link.
7. Disposable batteries.	Rechargeable batteries.
8. Majority of aids have no battery indicator to warn of voltage drop.	Majority of radio aids have a visual indicator to show when the battery needs replacement.

of hearing impaired children into mainstream schools. Lack of central government policy on funding for radio aids means that children are, in some cases, being expected to cope in noisy situations without radio aid equipment. Parents and teachers who want to find out more about radio aids, the types available, cost and practical handling should contact the National Technology Information Centre run by the National Deaf Children's Society (NDCS), situated in Birmingham. There is a free telephone line for parents: details are given in Appendix 1. The Centre lends out radio aid equipment on trial to parents and is very well worth a visit.

There are two types of radio aid systems. These are illustrated in Figure 3.11. In situation (a) the receiver worn by the child has two jobs to perform: it is the child's own personal body-worn aid and it is a radio receiver which picks up sound signals from the transmitter. In situation (bi) and (bii), the receiver passes the radio signal to the child's hearing aids via a lead or neck loop. The radio receiver does not change the child's own aids to make them any 'better' but it does transmit directly to the aids and so cuts out the problem of background noise. There are various ways of using a radio aid with post aural aids, via an audio input shoe, by direct input or with a neck loop. Neck loops are not as good as direct input using leads. With some older children a compromise has to be sought for a radio aid with neck loop is better than no radio aid at all. Children using their own aids with a radio receiver have the same quality and type of sound whether they are using the receiver or not. Children who use a radio receiver hearing aid all-in-one unit either have to wear the receiver all the time, or, more usually, change to post aural aids for use outside school. In this situation they may be presented with noticeably different quality of sound as they change from one system to another. All-in-one units have the advantage that for the more severely deaf child there is less chance of feedback at high power.

Radio aids are not 'the magic wand that will do the trick' as one mother thought, but they do have much to offer hearing impaired children. Simply providing a radio aid does not mean that a child will be able to cope in noisy situations. The way in which the aid is used is important; for example, the microphone on the transmitter should be situated within 6″ to 8″ of the speaker's mouth. Children can easily be cut off from conversations in the classroom and teachers will need to repeat comments made by

There are two types of radio aids.
The all-in-one unit (a) and the combined
system (bi) and (bii).

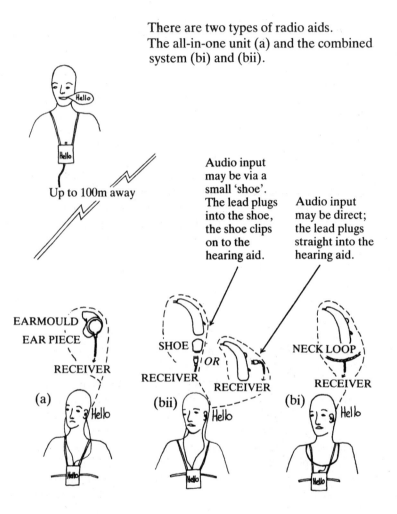

Up to 100m away

Audio input
may be via a
small 'shoe'.
The lead plugs
into the shoe,
the shoe clips
on to the
hearing aid.

Audio input
may be direct;
the lead plugs
straight into the
hearing aid.

EARMOULD
EAR PIECE

RECEIVER

(a)

SHOE
OR
RECEIVER
RECEIVER

(bii)

NECK LOOP

RECEIVER

(bi)

Three ways to receive 'sounds'

Combined radio
receiver and
hearing aid.

Radio receiver
directly connected to
behind-the-ear aid.

Radio receiver
connected to
induction loop
and behind-the-ear
aid switched to T.

FIGURE 3.11 *Radio microphone transmitter*

other children to ensure that the hearing impaired child is aware of other children's contributions. It is important to check radio aid systems regularly for faults. (An outline of fault finding is given in Appendix 2.)

The type of radio aid issued to a child in the UK will depend on a number of factors: the area he lives in, the types of radio aid already in use in that area, and the experience and bias of the professionals involved in the choice. Practically, it is easier to administer one or two systems in an area, particularly in terms of spares and repair procedures, than to have many different systems in use. If parents decide to purchase radio aid equipment themselves, they should discuss the matter fully with their audiologist and the teacher of the deaf. Costs of spares and repairs are high and if the aid is your property the cost of keeping the aid in work-

Remember to switch off the radio transmitter
or your child may hear some odd messages

ing order is also yours. It may be possible for parents to purchase a radio aid and donate it to the local authority for use with their child; in this way any further costs are covered by local services. Areas differ greatly in their practices, so find out what is going on in your area and ask questions. Contact the NDCS Technology Information Centre and ask their advice. The services are there for your child, so make them work for your child and help you. Finally, if you see a radio aid and are concerned about its appearance, take comfort from the thought that perhaps the age of personal stereos has meant they are not such a problem for children to accept. One grandmother wrote to us about her experiences:

> I took Joe on a local train to give him the experience of the railway. On the station a little boy stared at him and his radio aid, then asked 'why has he got that on?' I tried to explain that he couldn't hear and we hoped the aid would help him. 'Can he hear me talk to him?' was his next question. 'Unfortunately no', I replied. 'But just smile and say hello and he'll understand.' Whereon the boy patted him on the back and said 'never mind, you just go on listening to your music.'

Auditory Training Units

A typical auditory training unit is illustrated in Figure 3.12. Single units are frequently used at home by parent and child. They are commonly called speech trainers. In the school situation, a larger auditory training unit is known as a group hearing aid. As the name implies, in this case a group of children can use the equipment together; this provides an excellent link from teacher to children and between children. It also provides good amplification for the children of their own voices. ATUs provide the best quality of sound for hearing impaired children, amplification being provided over a wide range of frequencies. High levels of amplification can be used without feedback because the child listens through headphones. Speech trainers are often used with very small children because of the excellent quality of sound they give. Short daily chats about whatever your child is interested in, a teddy, a car, a sandwich or piece of old balloon, help to provide the basic foundations on which spoken language will be

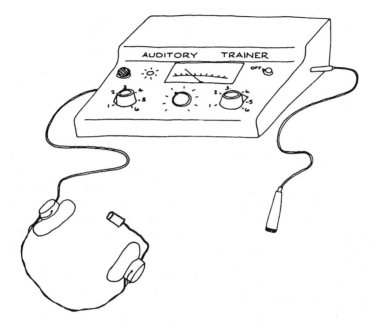

FIGURE 3.12 *Auditory Training Unit*

built. Your teacher of the deaf will be able to advise you as to the appropriate settings to use on the speech trainer and as to how it works. Group aids are found mainly in schools for the deaf and in some partially hearing units. Teachers and chldren are 'tied' to the unit by microphones and headsets. The increased use of radio aids has helped to make auditory trainers less popular because radio aids allow you to move more freely. However, radio aids do not have the quality of sound and high levels of amplification that ATUs have, but they are clearly more suitable in integrated situations. In the early stages, at home, speech trainers are a very valuable resource for parents and their hearing impaired children. If you have not been lent one by your teacher of the deaf ask about it. It gives the best sound you can offer to your child, but do not get carried away — they are not always convenient to use!

Infra-red Systems

These are primarily used in schools for the hearing impaired. Infra-red systems use light waves which are not normally visible to transmit speech sounds from the teacher to the children; the teacher wears a microphone and transmitter, the children wear a receiver. The child's receiver also has a microphone which picks up the speech of the other children. The receiver can be linked to post aural aids, headphones, or used to power a neck loop. It can also act as a body-worn aid. The main drawbacks of the infra-red system are that it cannot be used outside and it can be adversely affected by strong sunlight.

Electromagnetic Induction Loop

This system is commonly known as 'the loop' and is a cheap and relatively simple method of linking teacher to child. The teacher speaks into a microphone, either worn on the body or free-standing nearby. The microphone is attached to an amplifier, which also provides power for the loop. The loop consists of a wire which is placed around the entire room. When the teacher speaks into the microphone the sound is fed to the amplifier which drives the loop. The loop produces a magnetic field inside the room allowing the child's hearing aid, set on the T position, to pick up the message. There are several drawbacks to this system; for example, aids set on T provide a good teacher-to-child link but no child-to-child link. This system is also prone to weak or 'dead' spots. The hearing aid performance on M and T settings may be significantly different. Two adjacent rooms using the loop system may be affected by spillover from one system to another. As radio aids have been developed the loop system is now little used in schools; its main application is in some public buildings and in the home.

A full list of additional aids for the hearing impaired is included in Appendix 2.

Cochlear Implants

Headlines such as 'Bionic Ear for Birthday Girl' and descriptions such as 'miracle happens' and 'ecstatic parents' serve to bring false hope to many families with deaf children. A cochlear implant is a hearing aid, a part of it buried in the skull and part of it worn on the body. It does not restore 'normal' hearing or change a deaf child into a hearing child. A cochlear implant is illustrated in Figure 3.13.

Cochlear implants work by directly stimulating the auditory nerve with electrical sound messages. A microphone (1) collects sounds which are fed to the sound processor (2), where they are changed into electrical signals and passed to the transmitter (3). The electrical messages are sent from the transmitter to the receiver or decoder which is buried under the skin. The decoder (4) passes the electrical signal down the electrode (5) the the auditory nerve. There may be one electrode (single channel) or many electrodes (multichannel). Single channel implants are *extra*-cochlear; this means that the electrode is placed against rather than inside the cochlea. Multichannel implants are *intra*cochlear, the electrodes being placed inside the structure of the cochlea.

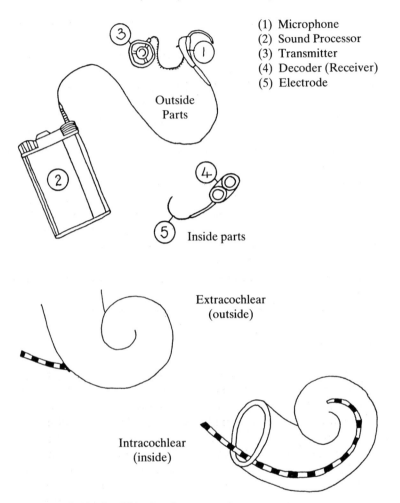

(1) Microphone
(2) Sound Processor
(3) Transmitter
(4) Decoder (Receiver)
(5) Electrode

Outside
Parts

Inside parts

Extracochlear
(outside)

Intracochlear
(inside)

FIGURE 3.13 *Cochlear implants*

The electrical message is transmitted from the electrode to the auditory nerve and this gives a sensation of hearing. The more electrodes there are, the more information that can be carried to the nerve of hearing. Someone with a multichannel implant will receive a more sophisticated signal than someone using a single channel input. This may possibly offer the chance for better understanding. In the UK single channel implants have been used until recently. These have advantages: they are cheaper, they are less invasive so that any residual hearing will not be further damaged and, most important in the event of mechanical problems, the single channel implant is easier to remove and replace. In some other countries, for example, Australia, the USA and West Germany, only multichannel intracochlear implants are being used.

The receiver and electrode are implanted under general anaesthetic in an operation which takes between two and four hours. This operation is technically straightforward and carries the normal risks attached to ear surgery — the possibility of complications related to the anaesthetic, post-operative infection and the risk of facial numbness. The implant will not work immediately; about four weeks after the operation the external parts of the system are introduced and the equipment is switched on. The 'switch-on' is closely monitored and controlled to ensure that the sound processor is tuned to the patient's needs. But this is not the end of the process: a profoundly deaf child with a cochlear implant is still a profoundly deaf child who will need specialist help, support and monitoring.

Different countries have different approaches to the problem of choosing suitable candidates for cochlear implants, but there are some general agreements:

1. Children should have a profound total hearing loss and get little or no help from the best hearing aids available.
2. In the UK only deafened children have been considered for implants. Memory of sounds is considered to be important if a child is to be able to use the electrical signals being fed to the brain. In some other countries prelingually deaf children have been implanted, notably in Germany, Australia and the USA; this is a very controversial area. Deaf adults, understandably, feel threatened by cochlear implants; they feel very strongly that the deaf children should make the decision for themselves as they get older.
3. There should be no history of recurrent ear infections.
4. Children should have good general health and accept that they are deaf. It is equally important for the child's parents to understand that their child is deaf and to accept it.
5. The child should have enough language to understand the operation and to give permission for it. He needs to understand that there will be some pain involved, and then lots of hard work after the operation.

6. The child's family are expected to be supportive and willing to learn about the implant and its workings, to take a full part in follow-up work and to understand the possibilities and limitations.
7. There must be an established and experienced cochlear implant team in the child's country of residence who can support the child and family.
8. Somebody must be available for day-to-day rehabilitation and to report back to the team if any problems arise.

If your child's situation fits into these categories and you want him to be considered for a cochlear implant, contact the Royal National Institute for the Deaf (address in Appendix 1). There are several unanswered questions which we feel it is important for you to consider. Cochlear implants are still experimental and whilst the implant team at the RNID are rigorous in their counselling and in choosing suitable candidates, this is not necessarily true of all centres offering implants worldwide. In the UK funding is from a charitable trust; in some places commercial factors may become important and this is not an ideal situation.

TABLE 3.2 *Number of cochlear implants in children*

	Age of implantee	
	2–9 years	*10–17 years*
Australia	19	11
USA	101	65
Germany	6	2
Norway	1	1

No one knows the long-term effect of stimulating the brain with electrical signals. This does not appear to do any damage, but much research remains to be done. Some devices do break down; the external components can easily be replaced but replacement of the receiver and electrodes requires a further operation. Clearly a cochlear implant will not work efficiently if there is damage to the auditory nerve or central processing area. There is a disagreement over the minimum age at which an implant should be performed.

In children the skull is growing and the effect of this on the implant and of the implant on skull growth is not known, nor the effect of middle ear infections on the implanted cochlea. The effects of electrical stimulation on remaining hair cells in the cochlea are also unknown. As we write this book the situation is changing rapidly as medical research pushes ahead. The statistics given in Table 3.2 were correct in February 1989. The total number of children between two and five years implanted within these groups is 70. As an aid to lipreading, cochlear implants may have much to offer in the future, but it will not mean that deaf children become hearing children.

The range of technical aids for the hearing impaired is expanding and in the near future there are likely to be some exciting and interesting developments. The important thing is for parents to understand what is most suited to their own child's needs and how to make the best use of what is available. Your child has the right to have the best. You need to ask and to ensure that you are given clear explanations so that you can use technology to help your child. It does not matter if you have to ask several times, you want the practical facts not the electrical circuits. Your child has to rely on you, the teacher of the deaf and the audiologist to get it right.

CHAPTER 4
Lipreading

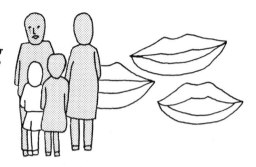

> To those who are deaf lipreading will become a strong part of
> their lives; in a way it compensates for the loss of hearing. We
> are often faced with situations where we have to rely on lip-
> reading. Many mistakes will be made, one learns by trial and
> error. The important thing is to check that your child has
> understood. (Comments from profoundly deaf adult.)

Lipreading is a skill. The less one is able to hear, the more one
needs to rely on lipreading. This does not mean that the deafer one
is the better one is at lipreading; in fact, research suggests quite the
opposite. Everybody will use lipreading to help them understand
what is being said in poor listening conditions, for example, in
factories, pubs and offices. All hearing impaired children need
to develop lipreading skills, and their parents need to be aware
of the practical limitations of relying on lipreading, to ensure that
problems are kept to a minimum. We have included some car-
toons of mistakes made by adult readers, embarrassing at the
time but funny to look back on. We hope these show the simple
mistakes that can easily arise and the need for patience and
a sense of humour! You can use a mirror to see how the mistakes arose. Say each phrase or sentence and see how similar they
look.

Problems Arising in a 'Normal' Day

We both feel that all children enjoy communication with
those around them and that children deserve to be included. The
following description of a day is not meant as a catalogue of potential disasters but a brief reminder of practical situations where
lipreading alone is a problem.

If you've finished with the paper,
I'll throw it away!

If a child cannot see you he cannot lipread you. On waking up, whilst not wearing his hearing aid there will be no chance of communicating by speech until your child can see you. Distances of up to three metres have been found to be acceptable for lipreading; clearly with a small child, one metre is more practical. So, after waking up, it is night clothes off and a good wash. No lipreading whilst the face is being scrubbed or the back rubbed but plenty of opportunities in between! Back to the daily routine — getting dressed. It's hard to chat naturally, bearing in mind that the hearing aids may not be in yet and your child's head has disappeared as he struggles into a sweatshirt or pulls on his favourite stripy socks. Now the hearing aids are in, so there is at least a definite point of contact, and it's downstairs for breakfast. Your child cannot lipread in poor light, walking down the stairs for example, or whilst you are eating your toast or anything else! Brushing hair and teeth, particularly in the case of a toddler, may be a struggle in itself so do not expect your child to lipread what your plans for the day are at the same time.

A small child playing on the floor whilst you wash up and cope with the daily round of housework may have a few problems. You are a moving target to follow as you dart around the house; a sharp angle and pain in the neck as he looks up at you from the floor; and lighting for lipreading is poor. If you stand in front of a window the light behind you puts your face in shadow, making lipreading very difficult. A trip down to the shops provides lots of possibilities for chatting together but not if the pushchair faces away from you, or if your child is fascinated by a toy in the pram or if he is struggling to escape from reins or your grip. This does not mean that you should not talk, but be realistic in the response you expect. The more chances a child has to experience language the more chance he has to learn to lipread. At least supermarket trolleys have the seat facing towards you and the child at a good height so there's a good chatting situation!

Playgroups and toddler groups have lots to offer any child. As your child scoots round on a tractor, fights his way on to the trampoline or wrestles a toy from his best friend he is not going to be looking at you or anyone else for a clear lip pattern. Situations will arise when he does need to understand what you are saying: drink time, story time or being removed from a toy somebody else is using. Remember that how you look says a lot about how you feel. Shouting makes you look angry whether you are or not! Home for dinner, and a full mouth or chewing make lipreading impossible. Do not be put off, there are still lots of opportunities to chat at the table.

If a friend with other small children calls round remember that your child may well have difficulty in knowing who is talking, and so trying to follow a conversation can be problematic. Anything in front of the speaker's face obviously will present a problem for the lipreader.

A child who is watching his favourite television programme is unlikely to appreciate you leaping between him and the screen to ask if he wants a drink. A light touch on the shoulder or flashing the lights will draw his attention to you. This will, of course, depend on the child's personality — many hearing children seem to 'lose their hearing' when watching the television.

At teatime there is a 'tennis-match' situation, looking from one person to another to follow the conversation. Try to be patient. It will help if there are clues to 'cue in' the deaf child. If a brother or sister has some news, try to ensure that there is some way of including the deaf child. Any object, quick sketch, mime, whatever your child needs to include him, will stop the frustration of being excluded. This is most important. We are not suggesting that every time the family is together is has to be an amateur dramatic production. The rest of the family need to be able to talk freely and easily about their day.

Sometimes when you really want your child to lipread he can't because he is frightened, distressed or angry. This can be frustrating, but remember that a child cannot lipread through tears. A soothing hand, firm cuddle or simply being there will reassure him until he is able to control his tears.

A bubbly bath full of toys and your grubby child — now lipreading is important because hopefully you have removed the hearing aid before he climbed into the bath! Bedtime stories are important for all children; do not forget that the position of your hearing impaired child needs to be carefully considered.

It is very important to remember the needs of brothers and sisters who also want to have your attention at bedtime. They have just as much right to your time and understanding. As the children are tucked up in bed, one final thought; once the lights are out there is no point in discussing the plans for tomorrow, giving a few calming words, or saying you love him. No one can lipread in the dark.

In the school situation, part of the teacher of the deaf's job is to explain to other teachers about the special needs of deaf children: the problems of assembly in the hall, class discussions and games lessons, of the teacher talking whilst writing on the board or walking round a room. Children can and do become very adaptable and astute lipreaders and many will cope well in difficult situations.

Many people try to help lipreaders by either overmouthing, giving a very exaggerated pattern, by shouting or by using as few words as possible. None of these help the lipreader. Children need to learn to lipread the general public so that as they grow up and become independent they can carry on with their own lives. Children who are given exaggerated lip patterns are given an abnormal view of speech which does little to help them. In a similar way, shouting exaggerates the pattern and causes distortion in the hearing aid, so it is best avoided. If you say *'Dinner'* rather than saying *'Dinner's* ready. Come on, it's *dinner* time. Wash your hands then sit down for *dinner'*, you may be trying to help by concentrating on the important word. In fact what is happening is that you are reducing the amount of information available and making it harder for your child to understand. He suddenly hears one word and has only one chance to lipread. If you put the word into sentences you give more to listen to, a better chance of making sense of the message and, in this case, three chances to lipread 'dinner'. If your child looks totally lost, give him a clue. Imagine how you would feel in a foreign country listening on a poor telephone line and then think of your child trying to understand you, using his hearing aid and lipreading. It is not always easy to be patient but it is easier if you understand some of the limitations inherent in lipreading.

Each sound is unique, different from any other sound. It is these differences between sounds, and the way sounds go together, which make it easy for normally hearing people to understand speech. The ear is sensitive to each separate sound unit and can easily distinguish between them. Each sound does not have its own individual shape in the mouth; in fact, many sounds look identical and the eyes alone are unable to separate each sound. It has been estimated that up to 60% of sounds in English cannot be individually identified. Additionally some sounds are impossible to lipread because they are made at the back of the mouth, for example, 'g' as in 'goat' and 'k' as in 'kite'. Other sounds look identical: 'p', 'b' and 'm' as in 'pat', 'bat' and 'mat' are good examples.

A hearing impaired child, when first seeing you say the word 'banana', could easily think it was any of the following words:

banana	manala	malana
balala	palala	palana
manana	panala	balana

This is where consistent use of good hearing aids will help children to identify the correct word, by using the clues they hear as well as those they see.

The most important factors in understanding speech through lipreading are the linguistic aspects of words. The more one knows about language the easier it is to lipread, just as the more one knows about cooking the easier it is to produce a meal. 'Normally' hearing people are able to talk and communicate without understanding the way language works. A competent three-year-old can apply complex rules with no knowledge of linguistics whatsoever. One hearing child on holiday in Belgium performed a dance; an adult watching commented *'C'est magnifique!'* (It's great). The child knew no French so she simply made sense of what she heard — 'C'est magnifique' was changed to 'Mind your feet' which she then said every time she danced. All languages have rules — the way words are put in a sentence, the part of speech used, the sounds used in that language and the way sounds are put together. Consider these two questions:

Why don't we go to the park?
To we why park don't go the?

The first sentence is straightforward to an English speaker; the second is harder to make sense of but not impossible. The words are still English, all the sentence is there but in the wrong order. The question mark gives us an excellent idea of how the words need to be combined to make sense. If we use the same words but combine them into non-English letter groups then meaning is lost, even though all the letters are present:

Wat gkoh ow otd pyne tehr?

The only linguistic clue left is the question mark. Unfortunately now we have no idea what the question was.

Vision alone provides an inexact and problematic channel in the understanding of speech. Use a mirror to compare the shape of these two sentences:

She can have mine if you like.
He's going on his bike tonight.

Visually there is little to choose between these sentences. Context is a great help to the lipreader, as the topic of conversation is often limited by the situation. It would differ in a shoe shop, a local supermarket, the hairdressers, at playschool or the local library. The type of language used also varies with the situation. Discussing a child's toy does not require the same language as a visit to the local doctor or complaining to a sales assistant. We all change our language in different situations and these changes give clues to anyone who has to lipread. In order to lipread a message, a good understanding of language is needed, but, conversely, in order to understand language, severely and profoundly deaf children need to be able to lipread. The task these children face appears daunting but it has a humorous side too. One deaf pupil was studying *Macbeth* at school. The teacher explained the witches' curse that would befall the Queen's baby if it was born naturally. She explained that the Queen had a Caesarian delivery, and was helped by a *surgeon*. At this point the problem began — how could washing the baby in *detergent* save it from the witches' curse? Suddenly the scene was transformed from Macbeth's castle to a luxurious bathroom, lots of bubbles and a very clean baby. Confusion between the words *surgeon* and *detergent* changed Shakespeare's scene completely.

If you think back to your own school days there were probably lessons when you listened but looked out of the window, or half listened but thought about something else. Your hearing generally let you get away with not fully attending. A hearing impaired child has to pay attention all the time if he is to understand. It is hardly surprising if he is tired at the end of the day and wants a rest from lipreading. A child who refuses to look at you may be being difficult or may simply be exhausted or confused. Getting upset about it will not help.

Strangers have different accents, rates of speech, turns of phrase and different faces. In this situation a little extra time and patience are important for the lipreader. He needs time to cue in to new speakers and different speech patterns.

Finally, something which is very simple and easily overlooked is that a child needs to be able to see properly if he is to lipread. A sight test should be carried out to ensure that your child can see normally; if not, he should have the appropriate spectacles fitted.

Points to Remember

1. Lipreading involves guesswork, it is demanding and problematic.
2. Shouting, mouthing speech or exaggerating speech sounds all make lipreading more difficult.
3. Speech should be kept at a normal rate; slightly slower is fine but the slower speech becomes the harder it is to understand.
4. Anything which obscures a speaker's face causes problems for a lipreader.
5. Be prepared to repeat things, reword them, use objects, gestures or signs to help with understanding.
6. Ensure there is good lighting and that the light is on the speaker's face rather than behind it.
7. When you are reading a story or sharing a toy allow your child enough time to look at the book or toy before you expect them to be interested in looking at you. They may have enough hearing to look and listen, they may learn to use their residual hearing to the absolute maximum. Hearing impaired children need your informed understanding of their situation.
8. Remember — your child wants to understand and your patience and help will give them the confidence to guess if unsure.

FIGURE 4.1 *Why do you think it would be hard to lipread these people?*

Why do you think it would be hard to lipread the speakers in Figure 4.1? Answers:

a. Flashing disco lights.
b. Sun behind the speaker, face in shadow.
c. Speaker too far away.

d. Speaker too close; no one likes to see how many fillings you have.

e. Dangling earrings and heavy make-up can be distracting for the lipreader.

f. No one can lipread the back of your head!

g. Eye contact is lost when the speaker is wearing sunglasses. It also can be distracting to see one's reflection in mirror-type glasses.

h. Munching an apple, or chewing gum, can make it difficult to lipread.

i. Over-grown beard or moustache or both.

j. Mumbling, or fingers in mouth, looking downward, with hair covering the face.

k. No one likes looking through smoke.

l. Like watching Wimbledon, three speakers at the same time — who's talking now?

CHAPTER 5

Language Development

> Communication is the breath of life. It helps to build up language and with language you can stand on your own two feet. (Profoundly deaf adult, educated orally.)

> To us the turning point was when we realised that it was communication that was really important. (Father of a profoundly deaf child using Total Communication.)

> Families with no communication are broken families. (Mother of four severely deaf children, all attending the local mainstream schools.)

> Take an interest in our child as a human being and make sure they acquire a way of expressing themselves. (P. Ogden and S. Lipsett (1982), *The Silent Garden: Understanding the Hearing Impaired Child.*)

Language is something we all have in common. It allows us to express our thoughts, to develop our ideas and beliefs, to share feelings, to share the ideas of the past and to plan for the future. Everyone we interviewed for this book expressed the same belief — communication is the focus of our lives as human beings. The way in which people communicate, the language they use, is not the most important factor; rather, it is the ability to communicate effectively. There is no doubt that spoken language is the most useful form of language because it is most used and most easily understood by the population at large. This does not mean that sign language is in any way inferior. The route to take your child along is up to you. The goal is for your child to develop language in order to communicate with anyone he chooses to; how this is achieved is your decision. Professionals argue about the best route. We feel that parents need to understand about language development, about hearing loss and about sign language without the pressure of an involved and committed professional breathing down their necks. Ogden and Lipsett, in their book *The Silent Garden,* express our feelings clearly: 'In your home, free from prejudice and with imagination, you can create an environment in which ideas and information flow freely by whatever means of communication necessary to get them across.'

The subject of communication is covered in this and the next two chapters. This chapter first looks briefly at language development in normally hearing children; Chapter 6 looks at sign language and manual support systems; Chapter 7 looks at music and music therapy for hearing impaired children. All these subjects have a vast amount of literature written on them. Our intention is to give you some basic information and some references for further reading.

Development of Spoken Language

EARLY DAYS

All children want to communicate; having 'normal' hearing or a profound hearing loss makes no difference to this. Deafness does not take away the desire to communicate, but it does affect hearing and speech. No child born deaf mourns their loss of hearing, though parents may mourn on their behalf. The child is far more interested in all the exciting things to be seen and explored, facial expressions, natural gestures, movements that can be seen. All babies develop a considerable range of non-verbal (unspoken) language skills. Sometimes these non-verbal skills are unrecognised by hearing adults simply because speech is relied upon as the main source of information. Non-verbal features play a very important role in communication between hearing people; a smile, a wave of the hand, an aggressive stance, all say a lot about how people feel and communicate those feelings to other people. The ability to use and to understand non-verbal communication enhances both spoken and sign language, but does not replace either of them.

In the early days babies are passive communicators; crying results in parents taking action but the baby is unaware of this relationship. Between the ages of two and four months babies respond to the tone of voice used or the facial expression seen; thus a gentle, soothing voice and calm expression will produce a different reaction to a sharp, annoyed voice and angry face. Parents are natural communicators; without thinking they provide their child with a vast experience of language. The majority of parents are unaware of their own skills. Most parents do the right things instinctively. Parents realise a baby will not talk back, yet mothers are known to have long discussions with their babies, providing both sides of the conversation, offering a wealth of facial expression and movements, asking questions and leaving suitable pauses before filling in gaps.

'I'm coming, it's alright, well what a big cry! What's the matter? Are you thirsty little one? Come on, up to Mummy. Come and have a drink and a cuddle with me.' (after D. Crystal, *Listen to Your Child* (1986).

FIGURE 5.1

David Crystal, in his book *The Cambridge Encyclopedia of Language* (1987), notes that mothers are naturally very adept at varying their language to fit with the child's stage of development. Figure 5.2 summarises these reactions. The baby is not intentionally communicating but the mother's responses help to shape the baby's actions and encourage future communication.

So what of the hearing impaired child? For the majority of children hearing aids are unlikely to be fitted as early as this. In terms of sound, the amount they hear of their parents' voices will vary from almost all to nothing. Yet even without sounds a lot of communication is going on already. Look back at Figure 5.1. The mother is talking to her baby and is saying a lot, but the message is also in her whole appearance, a smile, a welcoming face, out-stretched arms, the way she is standing. Once the baby has been picked up a new range of clues are available, even to profoundly deaf babies. The rhythm of speech can be felt and facial changes, raised eyebrows, smiles, frowns and moving lips can be seen. For children with a less severe hearing loss, close proximity means that some of the sounds of speech will be heard.

	Smile (5 weeks)	Cooing (2 months)	Laughing
Mother's responses	lively, excited	soft voice, gentle	varied response according to situation

FIGURE 5.2

MOVING ON

A big change comes when babies deliberately try to com-municate. They begin to realise that actions produce responses: 'If I do this, that will happen.' In their excellent book *Let's Talk* (1986), R. McConkey and P. Price provide a list of the many ways in which babies communicate their feelings and needs. Some of these are illustrated in Figure 5.3. The important thing, especially if your child has a hearing loss, is not to ignore his attempt to com-municate. Encourage him to communicate with you. As many parents at this stage are unaware that their child has a hearing loss, it can be a very frustrating and disappointing time for parents. Hearing impaired children are likely to have difficulty in understanding situations because they are unable to hear the tone of their parent's voice, and without facial clues, an annoyed or worried expression, miss the point. Parents are surprised or even annoyed by the child who, despite repeated warnings or exaggerated speech, apparently ignores them. For example, as a child reaches for a plug the mother might say, 'No, mummy said NO' (child 'ignores' mother) '*NO!* it will hurt you, come on, come away. NO!' The mother's speech is likely to go from a gentle but firm 'no' to an exaggerated emphasised 'NO' and finally to an annoyed '*NO!*' The child, unaware of his mother's warning, carries on exploring this exciting shape in the wall, and is suddenly surprised by his mother who picks him up, looks very angry and deposits him some distance away. The child is frustrated and shocked by his mother's sudden movement, the mother is annoyed that her child is so wilful and will not listen to her. It is very easy for communication to break down; parents, like everyone else, like to see responses, they want to know their child is interested in them. Poor, infrequent, or total lack of response to the spoken word can, understandably, lead parents to giving up. 'There's no point in talking to him, he never listens anyway.'

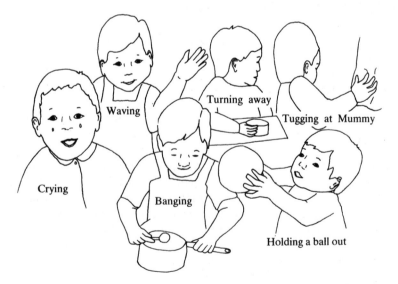

FIGURE 5.3 *Different ways of communicating*

Hearing impaired children miss many of the basic spoken language skills because they hear incomplete or distorted sounds, or only a few sounds. But sounds alone do not make language, so do not give up now! If you are aware of the problem areas you are also able to offer opportunities for children to develop missed skills and to learn new tasks. You will be able to encourage and value your child's efforts.

Looking

Parents help children to develop a variety of skills by the simple games they play with them. For example, the child bangs a toy — mother comments on the toy as the child bangs; or mother may look at a particular object and comment on it, 'ooh look at teddy, there he is. He's soft isn't he? Here he comes'. When a child looks at an object the mother will follow his action and look at the same thing. The hearing child can then look at the object and hear what is said; hearing impaired children also look but will not hear the comments the mother makes. The child needs to be able to look at the object, remember it and look back at Mum to have any chance of getting the message. This is a much harder task and a child needs to be more mature to cope with it.

Give a hearing impaired child time to look. Do not try to make him look at you. When he does look you can give him the information.
Speak clearly and simply to your child. Do not be afraid to use gestures to help you to get the message over, but most of all relax and enjoy your child.

Copying

All children love to play repetitive games, peek-a-boo, pat-a-cake, round and round the garden, and so on. All these are watched, giggled about and copied. These games are very valuable to your child so you have a good excuse for lots of fun together. Why are they important? Communication, amongst other things, is about learning to take turns, to anticipate actions and reactions and to respond. Every culture has its own wealth of simple baby games, nursery rhymes and finger rhymes that teach all these skills.

Daily routines around the house such as washing, dressing, mealtimes, shopping, housework, give lots of chances for copying and sharing; everyday chances to become involved. These are not simply chances for you to talk at your child; bombarding him with lots of complicated information is not the answer. Sharing things together involves much more than words. There is a sequence to events: for example, getting washed means going to the bathroom, putting the plug in, turning on the tap, finding the soap, getting hands wet, rubbing the soap to get a lather, putting soap on our hands and face, then washing the bubbles off before removing the plug and drying the hands and face — phew, quite a long sequence. There are lots of opportunities to show sequences, to give clear simple comments, to let the child join in and for you to accept their contributions. They can wash a doll or plastic duck and not only have lots of fun but practise the routine, see the pattern and understand the sequence of events. In their book *Let's Talk,* McConkey and Price give an excellent list of everyday activities which encourage turn-taking and other pre-verbal skills.

A child with a hearing loss needs to look at you when you are talking or signing, if he is to have a chance of joining in. Small children have their own interests, characters and tempers, so gaining their attention is no easy task. No child wants to be disturbed when he is busy playing. There is no reason why he should want to join in your game if he is already busy. Your interest must be focused on your child's interest. You should aim to be involved with him and take the opportunities that he gives you to join in.

Let your child control and focus your interest, then you can offer him your time, involvement and language.

You will be able to offer lots of opportunities to your child but you cannot demand his interest or insist on his involvement. Children learn many important things about the world around them by playing. Encourage them to explore things, the contents of the washing basket, the vegetable rack, the pan drawer, the toy box, everything around the home. A child finds out important facts

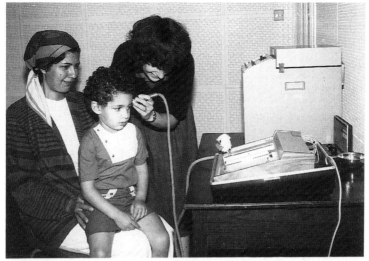

Impedance testing as part of a regular hearing check-up. (BRI)

Having a great time and learning together. (NAG)

Double the trouble? No, double the fun! (NAG)

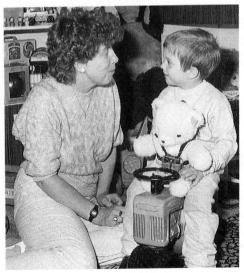

Teddy's got a hearing aid too.
(Breakthrough Trust)

Using a radio aid and watching carefully, will he win the game? (NDCS)

Signing — a part of everyday life for this mother and daughter. (Breakthrough Trust)

Lots to look at and lots to learn. (NAG)

Keeping in rhythm at music time. (NDCS)

David Hysslop using Vistel with a young friend.
(Breakthrough Trust)

about things by looking, touching, chewing, shaking and throwing. Exploration allows children to understand how things are similar and how they differ. Children need lots of experience of objects and an understanding of the object before they are able to put a label on it. There is a big difference between the thoughts of the two babies in Figure 5.4. This marks an important difference in understanding. Children are learning important facts without you — so, relax! You are very important but all children need to play by themselves. Your vital part in the language process is to follow your child's interest, to encourage your child's attempts, to incorporate simple repetitive games and tasks into the daily routine and to give up before the child loses interest.

FIGURE 5.4

Making Sounds

Deaf children smile, laugh and coo. They also babble but as there is no feedback without amplification this is where their own sound production stops. If a child is unable to hear the noises he makes he simply stops making noises. Partially hearing children will hear something of their own voice and will frequently go on to develop spoken language, although their speech may be unclear. Children with severe or profound hearing losses do not have the chance to develop speech unless they are provided with good amplification. Hearing aids and speech training units give the opportunity for these children to hear their own voices as well as the voices of others, and to develop spoken language. Clearly many important steps in the early language ladder may have been missed; early diagnosis and good parent guidance, together with responsive parents, are an excellent start but they are not the start given to the majority of deaf children even now.

Children learn about language using all their senses, but sound does have a particularly important role to play. Hearing people cannot shut sound out; they can close their eyes but not their ears. Like it or not they hear things around them and the sounds tell them about their environment. From within the womb babies hear, and, from the moment of birth, listen to the world around them.

Hearing impaired children have a lot of catching up to do in this area and they need your help to do this. Fortunately, the best way to encourage the development of spoken language is to use the natural skills that the majority of parents possess. As the parent of a hearing impaired child you will need to be more aware of your child's special needs. You may need help and encouragement in using your language skills, but do value your own contribution. You are of unique interest to your child and your child does want to communicate with you. Help him to develop his skills. Remember, it is important that all children's contributions to communication are valued.

Where do Words Come into This?

Words are very important; they are the units we use in spoken and written language to communicate. However, simply talking at children or giving them a list of labels (car, book, biscuit) will not encourage language development. This is not the way normally hearing people learn language and it will not help a hearing impaired child to learn language either. These children need all the fun, excitement and everyday experience of spoken language that all children have normally. They need to join in all the usual turn-taking games, the songs and nursery rhymes, the general chatter about the teddy or the contents of the shopping trolley, that other children enjoy. Certainly these children will need to use hearing aids and speech trainers and to be able to see you. These allow a hearing impaired child the optimum chance of being part of all the rich language experiences that exist in homes.

Much of our understanding of language comes from the tone of voice used. For example, the phrase 'Please put it down' could be said in a variety of ways expressing different feelings: *exasperation* — 'I've asked you to put it down ten times, now do it'; *concern* — 'Grandad, that is far too heavy, you will hurt yourself'; *delight* — 'my hands are covered in flour but the bouquet of flowers is lovely and can go here'; *fright* — 'that rat will bite you, don't be frightened but get rid of it'. So the way things are said is more important than the exact words we say.

Children will approximate what they say; that is, they will say what they hear. If they hear a distorted word they will repeat it in a distorted way; thus, 'biscuit' might become 'bibi'. Do not correct your child's attempts at speech — rather, try to accept and encourage. Simply saying 'Biscuit? Did you want a biscuit?' is far more helpful than saying 'Biscuit, listen *biscuit*, now you say it'. Nobody likes to be criticised.

> Continually breaking the flow of communication will put a child off rather than encourage him to have a go.

The most important information that is used in understanding speech is the time element. We talk in connected sentences rather than single words; the way that words are joined together is the really important feature of spoken language. These are the time cues. If the time cues are removed, understanding is lost, and for this reason it is vitally important that normal connected speech is used with hearing impaired children. By slowing down speech or talking in single words one effectively removes all the most important information and makes it harder rather than easier to understand speech.

There seems to be a lot to remember; and what's more, if all these things are just what parents normally do why make such a fuss about language and communication? The point is that hearing impaired children frequently miss out on early language skills and are unable to follow commentaries given by their mothers because they do not hear them. Copying and turn-taking may be harder to establish. Once a child is diagnosed as having a hearing loss and fitted with hearing aids parents can be encouraged to actively develop early language skills. The problem arises because skills which are often developed by passive non-mobile hearing babies may not be developed in active mobile hearing impaired children, who are more interested in chasing the cat than playing peek-a-boo type games.

So where do we start?

1. You must feel relaxed; take time to enjoy your child.
2. Focus on your child's interest.
3. Use clear simple sentences which relate to your child's interest.
4. Give your child a chance to join in, leave pauses, accept any contribution from him.
5. Use simple sentences which relate to your child's interests.
6. Avoid rambling on, long monologues and labelling — simply chat, remember you are talking to your child.
7. Use rhymes, singing and finger games with your child; there are tapes and books to help you.
8. When your child shows fear, pleasure, annoyance or understanding by his facial expression give him the words; comment on it, use his cues.
9. Ensure that your child's hearing aids are working properly. They will help him enormously. They are there to give your child access to sound, the sound of your voice and the world around him.
10. Despite all this, remember that the whole family demands your time; they can also be another source of help to your child and encouragement to you. Let them know that they are important as well.

Finally, beware that by actively encouraging the use of hearing aids you are not making your approval conditional — 'learn to talk and we can then accept you'. Value your child for himself.

CHAPTER 6

Sign Language and Support Systems

> If deaf people like it or not sign language is our first language, we see things visually. (A profoundly deaf adult brought up orally, now a strong advocate of Total Communiciation.)

> He has a natural feel for signs but doesn't like using them because they single him out as being different. (Mother of a profoundly deaf son.)

Sign language is a subject which arouses strong feelings in professionals and in deaf adults. Many hearing adults assume that all deaf children learn to sign; they also assume that deaf children cannot speak. Some professionals believe that sign language is a barrier to learning spoken language. Other adults believe that all deaf children should learn sign language. They are quick to criticise teachers of the deaf who cannot sign or who use a form of constructed sign language. We want to dispel some common myths, to explain what types of sign languages are in use, to report some results of children using sign language, and to look at the practical side of things for families who want to consider using sign language.

Some Basic Comments about Sign Language

1. Sign language is not English, French, Spanish or any other language put into sign. It is a group of languages in their own right with their own rules, structure and ways of expressing things.
2. Sign language is not a question of using the hands to make a *picture* of a word. A single sign may express a number of spoken words.

3. There is no international sign language understood by deaf communities everywhere. Different areas have their own sign languages.
4. The majority of deaf children are not taught sign language. It is estimated that at least 90% of all hearing impaired children have hearing parents and thus no immediate access to sign language at home.
5. Teachers of the deaf in the UK are not taught to use sign language as part of their initial training, although at present the majority of training courses do introduce trainee teachers of the deaf to sign language. On the other hand, in Sweden sign language is officially recognised as one of the native languages. Teachers of the deaf receive compulsory training in sign language as part of the their initial training.

A long and bitter argument has raged between the so-called 'oralists' and 'manualists' over the centuries. Research and new technology has helped in the understanding of sign language; this is leading to a more open and reasoned approach. Parents need unbiased information and support from the professionals, but this is not always what they receive: 'It is so unfair if new parents are faced with professionals arguing about the best method. Conflict is the last thing you need. Parents have to use their common sense and do what they feel is right in their home with their child.' (Mother of a profoundly deaf son.)

Essentially there are two types of sign language. One is the sign system used by the deaf community — British Sign Language (BSL), American Sign Language (ASL), Swedish Sign Language (SSL), and so on. The other type consists of manual support systems which have been developed by educators in an effort to bring deaf childrens' language closer to spoken language, be it English, German or another language.

British Sign Language

Sign language is a complex, structured language, a living language in the same way as spoken language. Just as new words come into use, so signs evolve and change over time, and new signs are developed. In Figure 6.1 the BSL signs for 'washing machine' are illustrated to show the change in signs as washing machines developed.

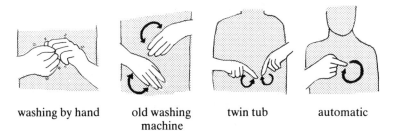

| washing by hand | old washing machine | twin tub | automatic |

FIGURE 6.1 *British Sign Language signs for 'washing machine'*

There are now signs for microwave and video; the sign for train has metamorphosed from 'steam train' to 'train' to 'high speed train' (we would need a video to illustrate this!).

There are regional dialects in sign language; this does not present a problem to the deaf community but may confuse those learning sign language. It also makes producing a general picture dictionary of signs a problem. Figure 6.2 shows some of the regional BSL signs used for the word 'white'.

Attempts to analyse signs in the same way as spoken language led many researchers to class sign language as inferior and simple. Videos have allowed a careful and systematic study of sign language and researchers now recognise sign languages as true, complex languages in their own right. Sign language has at last become respectable.

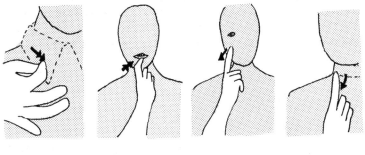

| white — collar | white — teeth | white — from an eye | white — from a reverend's collar |

FIGURE 6.2 *Regional variants of 'white' in BSL*

What Does Sign Language Involve?

Sign language is a highly expressive language in which the whole range of emotions and feelings can be expressed. It is, of course, visual, but also three-dimensional and dynamic. It is not only two hands moving in isolation making a series of handshapes: sign language involves the whole person. Each person has a space around them, an 'empty box'. Within this they have the potential to use their own body, eye contact, facial expression, handshape and body position in order to communicate in sign. Anyone using handshapes alone is not signing, nor communicating. A hearing person may pick up clues as to a speaker's frame of mind from the worried tone in their voice, a suggestion of anger, and so on. A deaf person is constantly watching visual clues and making use of the body language we all transmit. The same sign can, in this way, be used in different ways: 'upset' becomes 'angry' by emphasising the hand movements more vigorously and by change in facial expression (see Figure 6.3).

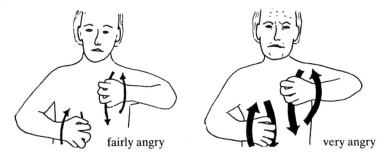

FIGURE 6.3 *Meaning is communicated using more than hand-shapes alone*

Context is also an extremely important feature of sign language, as it is in any other language. For example, there is no one sign for the word 'back'; the sign used would vary with the situation in which it was being used. Here are some examples:

Grandma's *back* is cold
Give it *back* to me
Put it *back* on the shelf again
She is at the *back* of the hall
Shall we *back* a horse?

FIGURE 6.4 *Signing space*

past present future

yesterday today tomorrow

FIGURE 6.5 *Time line*

A different sign would be used for 'back' in each of these sentences. You can see it is not enough simply to ask 'what is the sign for "back"?'

The structure of sign language is different from that of spoken language. Deaf people have a visual mind — they see what they want to say. A hearing person would see the situation in Figure 6.6 and say 'The ladder is leaning against the wall'; however, for a deaf person the ladder could not lean against a wall unless the wall was there first, thus in BSL the signs would be *wall–ladder–on*.

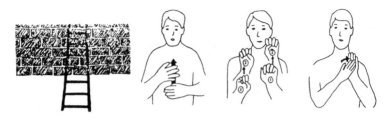

FIGURE 6.6 *British Sign Language: 'wall–ladder–on'*

Placement is another important feature of sign language. In describing who is giving to whom, the direction in which the sign for 'to give' is being moved is the information-giving item. This is easier to illustrate in pictures — naturally! (See Figure 6.7.)

As in learning any other language, the best person to learn BSL, ASL or any other sign language from is a native signer. Hearing children from a deaf signing family have no difficulty in becoming bilingual; they are fully competent in both sign language and the spoken language of the community in which they live. But as the majority of hearing impaired children are born to hearing parents they do not have a native signer in their family. The mother tongue is spoken rather than signed. This means that the involvement of deaf adults and deaf children will be very important if sign language is to be fostered.

Many educators express worries about using BSL. Sign languages, by their very nature, make it unreasonable to use speech

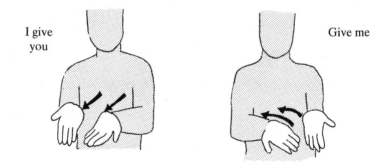

FIGURE 6.7 *The direction of the sign defines the direction of the giving*

at the same time. In this respect, the sign languages of deaf communities differ from the constructed sign support systems that educators have developed in an attempt to give deaf children spoken language. Consider the picture of the ladder leaning against the wall in Figure 6.6 and the order of the signs wall–ladder–on: the lip pattern and heard pattern would not match the visual pattern of signs. For a small child it would be rather like hearing French whilst lipreading Chinese.

Many deaf adults and research workers feel that sign language is the natural language of deaf children, in particular of profoundly deaf children. Deaf children think in pictures and have a natural ability to communicate visually. Sign language has a distinct advantage in the early stages of language development as children develop their ability to control their hand movements considerably before control of the voice occurs. Additionally, sign language offers complete, direct and immediate communication to a profoundly deaf child, in comparison to the speech heard which is distorted and incomplete. Researchers looking at vocabulary development have found that, in the early stages, children have a larger sign vocabulary than spoken vocabulary. For a profoundly deaf child a handshape can be demonstrated, fingers repositioned, movements copied with much more ease than spoken language. The development of good early communication skills is crucial to any child's development. Whilst profoundly deaf children may well develop excellent communication skills through an oral approach there is no way of predicting this scientifically within the first years of life. Sign language is a natural means of giving good communication skills in those years. This language base can then provide a means of learning spoken language.

Research from Sweden suggests that sign language alone can be used to communicate and build language for deaf children and that once they have sign language, spoken language can be successfully introduced. 'For Justin everything has happened since we started signing; if you watch him signing it is completely natural, it just flows from him.' (Parent of a profoundly deaf child.) Undoubtedly sign language has much to offer some families. The days when children signed in secret in the playground are gone; deaf adults are increasingly using their sign language skills in schools and homes; and many teachers of the deaf are being encouraged to learn about sign language and to develop their own signing skills.

Sign Language: The Bilingual Option

Many families are bilingual. The use of two or more languages in the home is seen as enriching the family. Parents are able to share a whole wealth of feelings, open the window on another culture, develop understanding of differences and similarities; children are encouraged to understand that differences are something to value and be interested in, rather than to be frightened of or antagonistic about. The idea of families with deaf children becoming bilingual, using sign and spoken language, was actively discouraged by professionals until recently. In the past there has been the ludicrous situation where children of deaf parents who use BSL have been forced to use spoken language in every situation outside the home. Interpreters were seldom available, even at important school meetings. Sign language was treated as inferior, a barrier to language competence. At last research is helping to make sign language respectable, and hearing families who want to use sign language are, in the main, being offered support and advice.

In homes where BSL or any other deaf sign language is the first language, language develops naturally. One of the problems the family may, sadly, have to cope with is the prejudice of professionals who place spoken language above sign language. Those teachers who are competent and fluent signers will have the knowledge and skills to encourage families. They will be able to accept the development of sign skills as a positive step towards language competence as a whole. Hearing parents are in a difficult position as their knowledge of sign language is likely to be non-existent.

In order for deaf children from hearing families to become bilingual in sign and speech there must be the close involvement of a native signer. This person acts as a language resource for the child and family, providing encouragement and signed input, monitoring and assessing the development of sign skills. The deaf instructor has a wider role and function within the family. Many parents have never met a deaf adult before, and they will have many questions to ask and possibly prejudices to overcome. A bilingual approach, by its very nautre, stresses the need for deaf adults to be accepted as individuals who have valuable skills to offer. Deaf instructors are skilled at establishing eye-contact and turn-taking and at adapting adult signs into baby signs. In addition to their many other skills, deaf instructors also give children a chance to see that it is 'alright' to be deaf. If children have never met a deaf adult it is easy for them to assume that everyone grows up to be hearing. Similarly, a deaf friend of the family can take pressure off a child who feels that spoken language is the only way to gain acceptance.

A bilingual approach involves close co-operation between deaf and hearing people whose joint aim is to nurture the development of a child's language skills, to monitor progress and actively pursue competence in language usage. Children have a right to master a language, to be able to express themselves clearly and to understand those around them. Research into bilingualism has shown that the ability to use one language well serves as the best base for learning another language. It actually makes learning a new language easier.

Opting for Sign Language — Practical Considerations

As stated earlier, it is important that the family have access to a native sign language user. These signers should have followed a course which helps them to be effective and sympathetic teachers. It is unfair and unwise to assume that all deaf adults are good sign language teachers: no one would assume that any hearing person can teach biology despite the fact that they can all breathe.

In one area of the UK deaf instructors are routinely used to introduce and support the sign element. Families are offered a short introductory signing course in their own homes. The deaf instructors visit over a period of six weeks and ensure the sign element is progressing.

When the time comes to deal with nursery placement the sign element is considered in relation to the child's overall language development. If sign is felt to be the dominant element then it is actively encouraged. The teacher and deaf instructor take over the sign element in the school setting; parents continue classes to develop their skills.

In some other areas sign classes, especially for parents, are held in homes or at schools. There are areas where there are no classes, where all children follow the oral/aural approach to learning language. If you feel that sign language is going to be important to your child you have two practical options — and a third if you are in crusading mood! If there are no schools using sign language in your area you can still choose to learn sign language. You must then hope, by the time your child is of school age, that his language skills will be sufficiently developed to allow him to join in fully. The local deaf club will run sign language classes; unfortunately these are usually aimed at adults and adult situations, rather than at parents of hearing impaired children. You could move to a more sympathetic area or decide that your child will have to board at a school where sign language is used. There are some exceptional parents who, against all odds, have managed to persuade local authorities of the need for a sign language element and have eventually met with some success. If there is no sign language element in the education available for hearing impaired children in your area, do try to meet other parents and discuss your concerns with them. They may be able to allay your fears and persuade you to have faith in the existing system. Similarly, they may give support to demands for a sign language element to be included in the future.

There are an increasing number of videos available for use by parents. Other resources are being developed, such as sign dictionaries; also, some bilingual books are now available using Signed English and English. Courses for families are developing. It is important to remember that sign language cannot be learned from a book; it is too dynamic, and the importance of movement and placement, of body language and use of emphasis cannot easily be illustrated on paper.

Sign language is a commitment. You cannot learn French or Russian in ten lessons — no one would expect to be able to, and the same applies to learning sign language. Many parents dutifully attend a short signing course and launch off into sign language at home. But, parents must be willing to go on learning sign and developing signing skills. You need to be a resource of sign language for your child, yet often the reverse is true — parents learn signs from their child. Parents must aim for a rich, expressive use of language to allow them to communicate freely with their child. Your child deserves more than merely the occasional sign added into your conversation, if this is the mode you have chosen in which to develop language skills.

Ideally, all the family will need to develop their signing skills. Children are usually very enthusiastic and expressive signers; parents may be more self-conscious and reserved at first. The pressure of time often means that it is the mothers who attend signing classes. In the home situation this can mean that all the problems, and all the fun, of having a child who is deaf fall on the mother. She is the only one who can communciate effectively. Sign language may open the world to a deaf child; it may close it to other members of the family, if the situation is not handled sympathetically.

Some deaf children find great difficulty in developing readily understandable speech. Sign language can help, not only in communication but in giving confidence. It is depressing to see a child struggling to communicate and having no idea what he is trying to say. For a child it can be very frustrating when his speech only produces puzzled looks and questions. Communication can quickly break down. If a child is able to use signs with his speech to 'cue you in' to what he is saying the benefits are twofold; you understand the message, and the child has confidence in his ability to communicate. You are also able to reply and give him a clear spoken pattern. Sign language is a rich and varied language which deserves the respect of all those involved with the education of the deaf. Researchers looking at the development of sign and spoken language have noticed that many of the milestones in development coincide; from 18 months onwards children start to put two words together or two signs together, for children given signs and speech develop the same skills but at a slightly different pace.

An exciting and interesting development is the research being carried out into deaf parents' handling of deaf children. Many differences have been noted in the deaf mothers' behaviour, particularly in gaining attention, the amount of language input, the use of gaze and visual interest tactics, and the use and manipulation of toys to interest and involve a child. These techniques are used naturally by deaf mothers whose experiences of the world give them an insight into the deaf child's viewpoint and special needs. At last in the field of deaf education the 'consumers' are being encouraged to help us all develop a better understanding of deafness and of language development, in both sign language and spoken language.

What are Manual Support Systems?

There are a number of manual support systems, some of which are considered here. They have all been constructed by educators in an attempt to help deaf children develop spoken language.

I believe in oralism myself through and through, but I think it must be supported. Total Communication helps to give meaning to language, hearing aids help with speech, fingerspelling to help signing to support lipreading to aid comprehension. (Comment from a profoundly deaf adult.)

The term 'Total Communication' describes an approach using residual hearing, speech, fingerspelling and signing together to support each other. The idea is that each child and family are offered the whole range of communication methods to establish both communication and language. Total Communication suffers from being a misunderstood term, interpreted in different ways by different people. In some cases it is a mixture of BSL and speech, in others it is Signed English and speech, and so on. Ensure that you ask precisely what is meant if Total Communication is suggested for your child so you know exactly what it will entail. It does offer flexibility of approach, using all the important means of communication to help the child develop language skills.

One partially hearing unit changed from an oral approach to a Total Communication approach in an effort to meet the special needs of the profoundly deaf children attending the unit. The effects of introducing Total Communication were monitored and the following results noted:

a. A noticeable improvement in the acquisition of language skills.
b. Significant improvement in speech skills and motivation.
c. Attainment of reading ages at hearing peer group level.
d. Total Communication appeared to encourage social development both at school and at home.

The teacher of the deaf involved in this project felt that Total Communication gave children the chance to learn to read, acquire number skills and join in with the communication going on around them according to their general ability, not according to their lipreading ability or speech skills.

FINGERSPELLING

Fingerspelling is a signing system where each letter of the alphabet is given its own sign (see Figure 6.8). Fingerspelling is quick to learn and very flexible — any word which can be written down can be fingerspelt. It is useful for signing names, or for words

FIGURE 6.8 *The British Fingerspelling Alphabet* (reproduced, with permission, from *Communication Link, Directory of Signs*, published by Beverley School for the Deaf, Middlesborough).

where there is no sign available. However, for small children, who are as yet unable to spell and have difficulty in controlling precise hand movements, fingerspelling is not ideal. Another drawback is that handshapes, even close up, can be easily misread. It can be difficult to become proficient at reading back fingerspelling. There is no international alphabet for fingerspelling; the British use a two-handed system, Americans and people of many other countries use one-handed systems. In general, fingerspelling is a very useful tool; it bridges the gap between the spoken words, signs, and the written word.

SIGN SUPPORTED ENGLISH

In Sign Supported English (SSE), the key words in the sentence are included and signed in English word order. BSL signs are used together with speech. Children often start on Sign Supported English and as their skills develop they move on to Signed English and begin to use the grammatical markers. In Figure 6.9 the example of 'The ladder is leaning against the wall' is now signed using some BSL signs but with English word order. English grammar is introduced.

| ladder | is | leaning | against | wall |

FIGURE 6.9 *A sentence in Sign Supported English*

English-speaking parents often find that SSE offers them the most effective route to the introduction of signs. As SSE allows parents to use their own language together with signs it is relatively quick and easy to learn; and as they are no longer caught up in a 'foreign' language parents are able to concentrate on their child rather than on the construction of sign language. Signs are often more easily assimilated in a relaxed and natural situation. SSE can offer a bridge to BSL; parents are allowed to be in control of the sign component and deaf children are allowed access to signs and thus eventually to BSL.

SIGNED ENGLISH

This system is a teaching tool rather than a sign language proper like BSL. It presents signs in English word order. There are fourteen different sign markers which are used to show important parts of grammar, such as past tenses, plurals and possessives. The sentence 'the ladder is leaning against the wall' is illustrated in Signed English in Figures 6.10; it shows the BSL base together with addition of grammatical information. Note how the word order has changed from the original BSL (compare Figure 6.6). Note also that the word 'against' is fingerspelt; this ensures that

| the | ladder | is | lean | i-n-g |

a-g-a-i-n-s-t

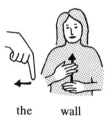

the   wall

FIGURE 6.10 *A sentence in Signed English*

the correct preposition is communicated. It is essential that speech is not distorted by slowing down to fit in with signs, for this removes vital information that is essential for comprehension of spoken language. Signed English is always used with speech; the markers help to identify important aspects of spoken language which are lost in lipreading. In order to use Signed English parents need a good base of BSL sign vocabulary.

PAGET GORMAN SIGNED SPEECH

In Paget Gorman Signed Speech, signs are used to represent each word that is spoken, together with the grammar of English. The system has 37 basic signs: for example, colour, animal, time, position. Each time there is a related sign, the base sign is used together with an identifying modification. For example, the basic sign for 'time' would be used as part of the sign for all the following words: now, tomorrow, late, evening, Christmas, soon, and many more. PGSS is always used with speech and is only taught by qualified users. The flexibility of this system means that it has been used with a wide variety of children who have communication problems; originally devised to use with hearing impaired children, it is now also used with children who have cerebral palsy, aphasia, mental handicap and by some children who are deaf and partially sighted. PGSS was the first sign support system, in recent times, to be widely accepted in schools and this did much to open the door for the whole range of sign support.

Figure 6.11 illustrates the 'wall' sentence in PGSS. Note that the word order and grammar are English. Rather than using fingerspelling to show it, the '-ing' is added to the sign for 'lean'. Positions all have their own distinct signs: thus 'against' is signed rather than fingerspelt.

CUED SPEECH

Cued Speech is an oral method which uses a set of hand cues with speech. The hand cues are used near the mouth to overcome the problem of lipreading, where so many sounds are identical or impossible to see. The system was devised by R. Orin Cornett, and has been adapted for use in over thirty languages. The aim of cued speech is to provide an accurate way of communicating speech, by overcoming the ambiguity of lip patterns. There are eight hand shapes used to show the consonants of English; consonants which look similar have a contrasting hand cue. The sounds in each cueing group look very different on the lips, so using lip pattern and hand cues it is possible to identify all the sounds individually (see Figure 6.12). In one partially hearing unit, where cued speech was introduced, it was found to help the normally hearing children as well as the hearing impaired children. All the children showed an increased awareness of the sounds of spoken language.

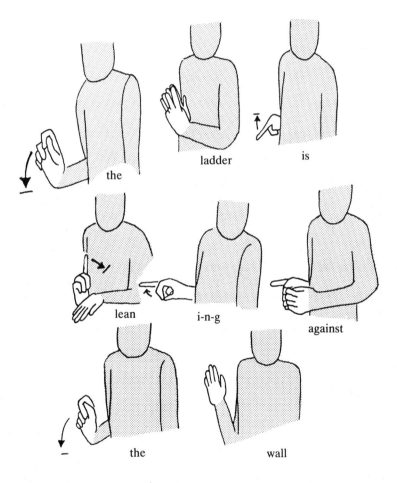

FIGURE 6.11 *Sentence in Paget Gorman Signed Speech*

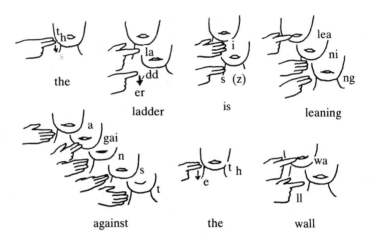

FIGURE 6.12 *Sentence in Cued Speech*

MAKATON

Makaton takes its name from the original team who introduced signs to help a group of mentally handicapped adults to communicate, MArgaret, KAthy and TONy. It consists of a restricted vocabulary of signs taken from BSL; no attempt is made to include grammar. Makaton is used primarily with children and adults whose learning difficulties make it extremely hard for them to communicate even simple ideas. Makaton has helped to give these people a means of sharing, of communicating their needs, wants and feelings, which might otherwise have been impossible.

Summary

No one likes to feel insecure or unable to express themselves. Every child deserves the right to a means of communication which he is relaxed and happy using be it the spoken word, sign language or both.

All children, once they start school, will be placed in either an oral setting, where spoken language is the norm; in a setting where oralism is supported by some kind of manual approach; or in a school where there is a 'Total' approach to communication using

BSL, SE, SSE, PGSS or Cued Speech. Your child's needs, and the provision available, will clearly play an important part in your decision about the mode of communication. No single approach offers a 100% guarantee of success for your hearing impaired child. Children learn in different ways, at different rates, and with varying degrees of success. But, at last parents are being offered alternatives; find out from other parents and professionals what alternatives are available for your child. The decision on which to use with your child is yours.

'My wife and I are making strenuous efforts to keep up with our son's BSL. We recognise the advantages of BSL but still, in many instances, resort to Sign Supported English' (quoted from the father of a profoundly deaf boy).

CHAPTER 7

Music for Hearing Impaired Children

For many parents the idea of music for hearing impaired students will sound odd, if not ridiculous. Some deaf adults feel that using music with hearing impaired children is merely an attempt to 'normalise' these children. So it is important to understand what we mean by music for deaf children, to consider how it is used and the effects that music can have on the children. It is not a question of passively listening to records and trying to follow a musical score, a task loathed by many hearing and hearing impaired children alike. Music for the deaf means, above all else, fun. It is also the chance to express feelings freely and to join in easily. Professionals have developed a number of different approaches to using music with the deaf, ranging from highly structured work using tone bars, to singing, dance, movement, work with instruments and signing to music. Note the spelling!! It is important for parents to be aware of the value of music and to value the contribution they can make at home. There are lots of simple ways in which families can be actively involved with music at home.

Why Music?

Music allows us all to express our feelings without using language. Lack of words presents no barrier to communication through music; watch any small child banging a drum and you will see clear evidence of this. Nevertheless, music and speech have much in common. They both require individuals to recognise, remember and imitate, sounds. Rhythm is vital to both, although in speech, hearing people give little thought to rhythm unless it is missing. All languages have their own rhythms, stresses and repetitions. Music, too, is characterised by rhythm, be it classical, rock and roll, or pop music. In all forms of communication, spoken, sign, and music, rhythm gives meaning.

The ability to differentiate sounds requires a number of skills. In music, the four most important elements are pitch, duration, intensity and timbre. These elements all have their counterparts in speech (see Table 7.1).

TABLE 7.1 *Comparable elements of music and speech*

Music	Speech
Pitch	The frequency, e.g. middle C (261.63Hz), a sound well within the range of most deaf children. Children may need help to place their voice.
Duration	Time factors, the difference between normal speech and slow exaggerated speech. These are the most imporant clues for understanding.
Intensity	How loud or soft sounds are. Vowels are naturally louder than consonants, and consequently more easily heard.
Timbre	Intonation, the rise and fall of speech. Children may not hear the rises and falls. They need help in recognising them and using them in their speech.

If hearing impaired children can learn to enjoy music, to relax and have fun, will music help in the communication process? Some exciting research was completed by Dr Margaret Tait in Nottingham, involving a group of profoundly deaf nursery-age children.

All the children showed similar degrees of difficulty in maintaining eye contact, making little use of their residual hearing and very limited use of their voices, and taking very little interest in being involved in conversations of any kind. Simple, repetitive songs were used with the children, both individually and in group situations. Music sessions included lots of actions, some props, a lively imagination and lots of singing. Tait looked at five areas in particular and tried to pinpoint the differences between ordinary conversation and singing, and the advantages singing may have to offer. Her results are summarised in Table 7.2. (For a full discussion of the research and findings, together with a selection of songs and hints, copies of Dr Tait's work are available: M. Tait (1985), *Reaching our Children through Song,* University of Nottingham.)

There seems to be little doubt that music has much to offer all hearing impaired children. The question for parents is, 'where do we start?'.

TABLE 7.2 *Children's responses to conversation and to singing*

Visual regard: Looking at the speaker
    In conversation — 40% of the time
    In song   — 80% of the time

Vocalisation: Making use of voice spontaneously to join in
    In conversation — 25% of opportunities taken
    In song   — 75% of opportunities taken

Voice quality: The actual sound of the child's voice

Rhythm: Children were almost 50% more rhythmic in song than in conversation.

Breath length: All children were found to have considerably longer average breath lengths in singing — two times longer than in conversation.

Modulation of pitch: Using the ups and downs of spoken and sung words.
        All the children used more 'ups and downs' when singing than in normal conversation: three times more in singing.

Auditory processing: Making use of the sounds that are heard.

Spoken 'test': The children with more hearing did very noticeably, and understandably, better than their deafer classmates.

Sung 'test':   All children did equally well on the sung test — this was a surprise and is the subject of further research by Dr Tait.

Memory: Did singing make information easier to remember? Recall of the 'plot', how much each child used his voice and the length of time he would talk without needing a contribution from the teacher, were all studied. In all areas children were at least three times better using a sung story than a spoken story.

Autonomy: Child's ability and wish to take control of the situation in conversation or through singing.

The children who were passive in conversation, making little or no contribution, were active leaders in singing sessions. They enjoyed the chance to control the teacher and their fellow pupils and to choose the songs. These children also used songs to take control at home; songs gave them the chance to feel confident and successful, to show off their ability.

Some Basic Ideas

'Babies and toddlers experience music most intensely through the physical and emotional contact they have with the people who care for them most closely' (S. Roberts (1987), *Playsongs)*. Relax, no one is testing you. To your child, your voice is the most interesting voice of all — so do not be shy, use it! There are some excellent tapes available; these are fine to help you learn songs and to give you confidence, but your own voice is far better for your child.

Make sure you are comfortable when enjoying music together. Young children love physical contact so singing with your child on your lap, in your arms, when you change him, bath him, anytime at all is fine. Begin with nursery rhymes, finger rhymes and peek-a-boo type games. Small children love repetition, and predictable plots. Peek-a-boo can be used to really emphasise face contact. Make use of hands, thin headscarves, tissues or newspaper to hide behind. Encourage your child to join in by popping a large handkerchief over his head then whisking it off as you get to 'boo!'.

Use movement, simple actions, rocking and bouncing, to emphasise rhythm and give your child a feeling of comfort, relaxation or excitement to suit his mood.

Use your own mouth to produce 'music'. Babble back when he babbles to you. Blow raspberries, especially against arms or legs — it tickles, and so always raises a giggle. Repeat and elaborate any sounds your child offers. Make the sounds louder and then softer, faster and then slower, raise and lower the pitch of your voice.

Help your child to control his breath by blowing bubbles or by blowing a windmill around. Bits of polystyrene or tissues can be used to have blow races across the kitchen floor. (Leave dried peas and straws until he is older, as they can cause accidents.)

Use household items, pans and wooden spoons are fine, for experimenting with rhythm. Upturned plastic bowls, tins and boxes all give different sounds and feel different to tap. There are almost endless possibilities for making your own instruments at home to bang, to shake and to scrape. Use them to have fun, to make noise and to show the difference between sound and no sound.

Simple songs have much to offer. It does not matter which songs you use. There are certain basic things to look for in choosing songs to get the most out of them:

> Look for simple repetitive phrases
> Look for repetition in choruses
> Use familiar vocabulary
> Be aware of lipreadability
> Look for songs with funny lines

(From Rita Keiner (1984), *Music for Deaf Children*.)

When you are sharing a book remember to include sounds for important objects or actions: a bark for the dog each time he appears; a *brrm brrm* for the motorbike; *boing, boing* as the ball bounces away. Use the same sounds each time so your child knows what to expect and can join in confidently.

There are many experts who have used their musical talents to help hearing impaired children to develop their individual skills through music. Father Van Uden in St Michielsgestel in Holland did much pioneering work; music is used with a whole range of children at St Michielsgestel, including deaf-blind and multiply handicapped children. Claus Bang, a teacher of the deaf and music therapist who works at the school for the deaf in Aalborg in Denmark, has developed a music therapy course for hearing impaired and multiply handicapped children. This is used in countries throughout the world. Claus Bang lectures widely, including annual visits to the United Kingdom, in conjunction with the Beethoven Trust. A major resource book for teachers using music with severely and profoundly deaf children was produced by Clive and Carol Robbins. In the United States, an exciting and innovative course in music has been developed at the National Institute for the Deaf, Rochester. There, Bob Mowers and Diane Habeeb have involved deaf students in all aspects of music including dance and musicals. In Brazil, musical skills are being developed through dance. Japanese deaf children are being encouraged to use music to help with rhythm perception in speech. Worldwide, music has been recognised as valuable to all children whether hearing or hearing impaired.

One very exciting and encouraging development over recent years has been the increase in musical performances by deaf students. One of these musicians is Paul Whittaker who graduated in music from Oxford University despite being profoundly deaf. He is an active supporter of the right for all hearing impaired children to have access to music.

Nina Falaise and Graham Howes teach dance to deaf children. They are both deaf professional ballet dancers. There are many notable others, using a variety of instruments and talents to give enjoyment to many, and fulfilling their own potential. Teachers have much to learn from these deaf musical specialists.

The approaches to music are many and varied, as are the teachers who use it. They all know of, and value, the contribution that music has to offer hearing impaired children. In your own home with your own child it is up to you. Have confidence in your abilities, share songs and rhymes together. If you are really stuck make a cardboard box 'cake', stick a candle in it and let every doll, teddy and cuddly toy have a birthday party. 'Happy Birthday' is the song almost everyone knows. You will be building skills for the future and giving your child the chance for fun and enjoyment with the most important person in his life — you.

CHAPTER 8

Educational Provision: What about School?

In deciding where your child goes to school there are likely to be three main possibilities, the local school, a special unit attached to a mainstream school, or a special school. Mainstream schools are the schools which the majority of children attend. Special units are given a variety of names, for instance partially hearing units, units for the hearing impaired, or resourced schools. These units are usually based within mainstream schools. Special schools are those which offer the maximum support in a setting which is outside the mainstream of education. Figure 8.1 shows the percentage of hearing impaired children attending each type of provision, from a survey of provision in England, Scotland and Wales in 1983 carried out by the British Association of the Teachers of the Deaf.

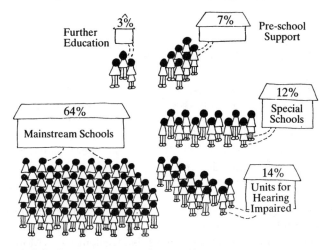

FIGURE 8.1 *Percentage attendance of hearing impaired children at various types of school*

Mainstream — Your Local School

Now the children are not bussed off to special Schools but are mainstreamed, expectation levels have been raised. (Head of Service for the Hearing Impaired.)

She is the only deaf child in the school . . . for Sofie it's her way of life. She's happy and enjoying it. (Mother's comments on profoundly deafened daughter, who is attending her local school half time and receiving individual help half time.)

Children may attend their local school and receive additional support from a peripatetic (travelling) teacher of the deaf or an assistant. The child is said to be individually integrated; he will probably be the only child wearing a hearing aid at his school. The teacher of the deaf will visit the school and offer specialised advice and support to the staff. Children may receive tutorial support, but the whole emphasis is on the child joining in with life at school. The teacher of the deaf monitors school progress closely as well as the use of hearing aids and radio aids. Children may receive visits weekly, monthly or termly but the teacher of the deaf can usually be contacted quickly should a problem arise. The majority of hearing aid users in England, Scotland and Wales (64%) are individually integrated into mainstream schools.

Units for the Hearing Impaired

I think Ann being integrated into a normal school is important. There is nothing crueller than children and Ann has to cope. Locking her away in a special school would have meant she had to cope with all of that when she left school. (Mother's comments on her severely deaf daughter who copes with the additional handicap of spina bifida in a Partially Hearing Unit.)

She did not fit in anywhere. She was desperate to go to the school for the deaf at that time. Things calmed down. Lisa is very settled now and her work is excellent too. (Mother of severely deaf child from a deaf family who now spends almost 100% of her time in mainstream education.)

Units for the hearing impaired have been, until recently, called Partially Hearing Units and thus are often referred to as PHUs. In this case children are based in a special unit within a mainstream school. Children will integrate, join in with the hearing children for some of their lessons. The amount of time any child integrates for will greatly depend on the child's abilities and needs. Children may be unit-based, so that the majority of their time is with the teacher of the deaf, or they may be class-based and then withdrawn to the unit for help in specific areas of the curriculum, for example language development and speech training. The teacher in charge of the unit considers each child's needs individually; it is her job to ensure that each child is integrated to suit his own needs and that suitable support is offered. She is also responsible for informing other staff of any child's special needs. A close watch is kept on hearing aids and radio aids, in ensuring that children and staff make the best use of the equipment available. At the secondary level, children usually spend the majority of their time in mainstream lessons and are withdrawn for tutorial support, allowing the teacher to provide extra help with problem areas, and to check on the child's understanding of different subjects. Units may be one room with one teacher or almost a miniature special school with several teachers. The vast majority of units are oral in approach as this is the approach used in mainstream schools, although recently some units have introduced sign language support for children. The type of unit available in any particular area of the country is unique in terms of its size, the school it is based in, the teacher of the deaf involved and the approach to integration. Originally only partially hearing children attended these units, but this is no longer the case; most partially hearing children are now in mainstream schools and units are catering for severely and even profoundly deaf children.

Special Schools

In the school for the deaf he's in an environment where he's happy. I'm happy for him to swim along. I don't want to make his life hard, I don't see why I should. (Father of a profoundly deafened son attending a day school for the deaf.)

We decided on a school for the deaf. There were three important factors in our decision: (1) the staff are well qualified and experienced in working with deaf children, (2) they use Total Communication which our son was using at home, (3) he would be in the company of other deaf children. (Deaf parents with a profoundly deaf son.)

Years ago, all hearing impaired children, whether partially hearing, severely or profoundly deaf, attended a school for the deaf. The move to integrate children into mainstream schools has caused the closure of some special schools and required that others become more specialised in their approach. Special schools offer the maximum level of support to a child. The school usually specialises in one particular area of disability, so there are special schools for the hearing impaired, for the physically handicapped, for the visually impaired and so on. Schools for the hearing impaired differ greatly in what they have to offer. Some are day schools where the children attend daily and are usually transported by taxi or special bus from home to school. Some are residential schools where accommodation is provided and children board there during term-time; pupils may go home every weekend, fortnightly, each half term or termly depending on location, the family situation, and the child's needs. Children who live near to a residential school may attend daily. Most schools for the hearing impaired offer some integration into local schools for their pupils. Children are integrated according to their own needs and abilities, but they are still offered maximum support within the special school, usually from qualified teachers of the deaf. For some children all their education is provided within the special school. The children will be taught in small groups using high powered amplification systems in acoustically treated rooms. The use of hearing aids, earmoulds and additional aids to hearing are all closely monitored. In addition, these schools often have other special resources, such as speech therapists and audiologists. Children who have additional special needs such as a severe visual impairment or physical handicaps will go to the school which can best meet their needs; in some cases this will still be the school for the deaf. A physically handicapped child with a hearing loss may well attend a school for the physically handicapped and receive peripatetic support from a teacher of the deaf. Each child's needs are considered individually and catered for in the light of what is available, and taking the parents' wishes into account.

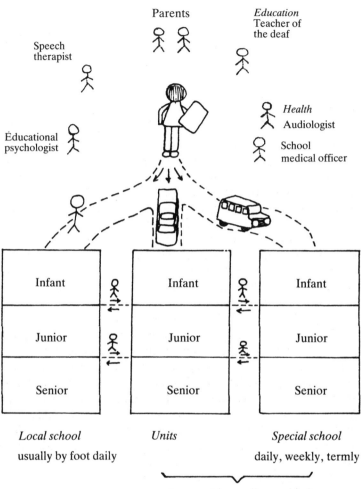

FIGURE 8.2 *Types of educational provision*

What about Pre-School Help?

Once your child has been diagnosed as having a hearing problem lots of new names and faces will come your way. Who are these people and what do they do? We have listed some of the people you might meet and there are others, though you might not meet all of them.

DIAGNOSIS

>   Family doctor and health visitor
>   Audiologist, audiological technician
>   Clinic doctor
>   ENT surgeon, otolaryngologist
>   Paediatrician

Well, that's just a start — the health services are there to diagnose
the presence of a hearing loss, and to tell you the the type of loss;
the severity of loss; if any medical treatment is necessary; to identify the possible cause of deafness and to prescribe and fit hearing
aids. The paediatrician specialises in child health and development.

FOLLOWING DIAGNOSIS

>   Teacher of the deaf
>   Speech therapist
>   Social worker for the deaf
>   Educational psychologist

The person whom you are likely to have most contact with is the
teacher of the deaf. The teacher will be informed of your child's
hearing loss and asked to visit you. The teacher of the deaf is a
specialist who is a qualified teacher and who has also trained to
teach children who have a hearing loss. She has a key role to play.
Ideally a balance of trust, confidence and respect is built between
teacher and parents and vice versa. Parents are very vulnerable;
there is often a feeling of resentment on the part of parents who
perhaps feel that the teacher is suggesting they are no longer able
to look after their own child properly. The teacher has a difficult
job. She must ensure that parents understand the audiological
information they have been given, that they know how to make
the best use of hearing aids, speech trainers, radio aids and more.
The first years of life are vitally important for any child. A child
with a hearing loss may fail to develop early language skills. All
parents are the natural teachers of their own children; the teacher
of the deaf is there to give advice and guidance as to the special
needs that arise because of a hearing loss and how best to meet
these needs.

The teacher of the deaf will know other parents in the area
who have hearing impaired children, and may well be involved in

running a Toy Library, Parents' Group or Music Group for pre-school hearing impaired children. The teacher will also be able to put you in touch with the local branch of the National Deaf Children's Society. Other parents are an important resource, as they have experienced many of the feelings you have had and situations that you will find yourself in. Their children may well already be at school and they will be able to tell you about the local schools and the options available. The teacher of the deaf will know what is going on in your area or whom to ask to find out. The other advice you receive will be related to your child's language development. The teacher will monitor progress closely and show you how to use your skills to the full. By helping you to understand and accept the implications of hearing impairment your teacher of the deaf aims to make you effective managers of your own child's development.

The other professionals involved all share the responsibility of informing parents of what is available, of their legal rights, of the child's special needs and of the best way in which they feel these needs can be met.

Speech therapists

Speech therapists have a wealth of knowledge about language development and communication skills. They may be involved in order to give help and encouragement in this area. Their focus is much wider than merely correcting speech sounds, which is usually felt to be inappropriate with small children.

Educational psychologist

The educational psychologist is involved in assessing the child's social, emotional and psychological development. Few psychologists use formal tests to assess children; the emphasis is on observing the child, on playing with him and in discussion with parents and teachers.

Social workers for the deaf

These are involved in supporting and advising families. They have a detailed knowledge of aspects as diverse as benefits available, the sorts of stresses which families find themselves under, and the technical aids such as doorbells and loops that are available. The social worker offers you the chance to talk freely about the pressures you may feel or your worries, and will help you to seek solutions.

FIGURE 8.3 *The path to education*

Statement of Special Educational Needs: What is it?

The 1981 Education Act applies to England and Wales. There are similar arrangements under another Act of Parliament for Scotland. The Act does not apply in Northern Ireland. The 1981 Act is important for parents as it directly involves them in the process of assessing their child's needs and in decision making. We are making only brief comment on this important Act because there are likely to be further amendments and changes in the law; we strongly advise parents to obtain up-to-date information from the head office of the NDCS. The main thrust of the Act is that wherever possible education should take place in a mainstream school.

ASSESSMENT

Children who are felt to have special educational needs have to have these needs assessed by the local education authority (LEA). The LEA takes into account the views of a variety of professionals and those of the child's parents. The object is to see the child as an individual person with a variety of needs: medical, social, emotional and educational needs are considered as well as any other factors the parents wish to bring to the professionals' attention. Parents are informed before the child is assessed and must, at the same time, be given the name of an individual who works for the Local Education Authority from whom they can get further information. Parents must be told that they can make their thoughts known either verbally or by letter. Parents have the legal right to the assistance of a friend or voluntary body, such as the NDCS, in putting their views. Most education authorities do their best to meet reasonable wishes of parents. The assessments aim to decide whether a 'statement' should be written; this is a legal document which states the child's special needs and which binds the authority to providing for these needs. The Act states that LEAs must ensure that children are educated in ordinary schools unless: (1) their special needs cannot be met there; (2) the placement will adversely affect other children in the ordinary school; or (3) it is an inefficient use of resources.

The following factors are important in considering which educational placement is best for a hearing impaired child. They are not listed in any particular order of importance.

1. Development of language and speech
2. Ability to communicate
3. Personality of the child
4. Type, degree and the age of onset of hearing loss
5. Parental views
6. Additional special needs, e.g. visual impairment
7. General mental ability.

No educational placement is permanent and statements of children's special needs have to be reviewed at least annually. If parents disagree with the provision made by the local authority they have the right to appeal, first to the LEA and if necessary to the Secretary of State. The Act gives parents the right to have their views taken into account, but it does not necessarily ensure that parents can send their child to the school of their choice. Your active participation in the statementing procedure will help to make sure you are fully informed and that your child is fully represented. Your opportunity is there by law; if you need advice and support ask for it — but do be involved.

Before School Starts . . .

It sounds obvious and simple: treat your hearing impaired child as a child first and foremost. It is very easy to let the idea of deafness cloud your judgement. Remember simply to ask yourself 'Would I let a hearing child do that?' If the answer is 'No' then it is 'No' for your child.

Do take time to relax and go out without the children. The longer you leave this the harder it will be to make the break when the time comes. Everyone needs time to relax, and once the school starts you will have to leave your child. Join the local babysitting circle, ask a friendly neighbour, relations or parents from the Toy Library to help out. Start with a short break if necessary, then gradually build it up to an evening.

Bedtime can be awful — we have some terrible memories ourselves. Deafness is not an excuse for not going to bed; try to stick to a routine, a quiet game, bath, clean teeth and earmoulds, story, cuddle, light out, sleep — sounds wonderful, doesn't it? Everyone has their own hints and tips: C. Green's *Toddler Taming — A Parents' Guide to the First Four Years* (1984) is particularly good. If you do start to feel that things are getting out of hand your educational psychologist may be a good person to ask for advice.

Unless a child is going to damage themselves or someone else ignore temper tantrums . . . and yes! we know it's hard. We also know of extremely large deaf adolescents who still have temper tantrums because parents have given in to their demands in the past. Be clear and simple in your response to requests. If the answer is 'No', stick to it, despite the screaming and kicking; just imagine him behaving like that at 14 and it may help you!

When They Start School . . .

Make sure your child has visited the school, met his teacher and seen his class. Scrapbooks made at home of birthday cards, cereal packets, sweet papers, postcards, bus tickets, photographs and so on all give the teacher a glimpse of the child's interests and a chance to make contact. Class teachers often visit the child at home which helps the child to see her as a friend as well as a teacher. Many schools are happy for parents to stay with their child for the first few days; this at least helps parents to feel more relaxed.

It may be hard to keep in close contact with the school if your child goes to a unit or special school. To overcome this problem most schools use home–school books; these are books where the teacher or assistant jots down a note about the day at school. This may include a picture, leaf, bit of material, photograph or new words. The book gives you an idea of what has happened at school, and you do the same about time spent at home. It is a parti- cularly useful way of passing on information between home and school and for encouraging back-up work too.

Children attending units and special schools usually have to travel by taxi or minibus. Sadly, many children spend an hour getting to school and an hour getting home, making it a very long day.

The type of provision in your local education authority will differ from the education authorities around you. Provision for deaf children differs far more from area to area than it does for normally hearing children. It is a good idea to find out about the facilities in your area; ask for a visit to be arranged and talk to other parents so that you are able to make an informed decision

HOME–SCHOOL BOOK

Sam went to the park with Daddy and Laura.

They had an ice-cream yum....yum.....

Monday
The park sounds lovely. Sam played with Asim in the house this morning.

We had music today
bang bang
toot toot.

FIGURE 8.4 *Example of a home–school book*

about your child's education. It is not unknown for parents to meet a deaf teenager with a rock bottom audiogram but beautiful speech, and for parents to believe that this speech is due to a particular educational system. Such parents may then opt for the same educational system which may turn out to be sadly inappropriate for their child.

Finally the time will come to leave school; for parents concerned about the distant future it is hard to know how provision will change and grow over the coming years and on into the twenty-first century.

After School — What Next?

By law, hearing impaired students, like their hearing brothers and sisters, are entitled to further education until their nineteenth birthday. Not all students wish to take up this option: some will leave school and go straight into jobs, some will be involved in training programmes. The amount of support available to hearing impaired adults leaving education varies. At present no one in full time employment is entitled to any kind of support, whilst those completing training schemes have statutory rights to some support. This situation is in a state of change. You are strongly advised to contact the NDCS, RNID or similar organisation in your country, to establish present regulations.

Those wishing to follow Further Education courses can choose to follow an ordinary college course where they will have the support of a Further Education Tutor for the Hearing Impaired. The tutor may be employed by the school service, the LEA or the college itself. Support may be given in a variety of ways including note-taking, interpreting, lipspeaking or sign support. Another option available is for students to attend a course specifically designed and run for hearing impaired students. These tend to be based in schools where hostel accommodation is available; students would be fortunate to find such a course in their home area. A third option can be for students to become resident in a school or hostel but to attend an ordinary college course. The staff at the school or hostel give back-up work in the evenings. The students also have the opportunity to make social relationships with other hearing impaired students following similar courses and are not so isolated as they might be at a local college.

Students who wish to follow higher educational courses at polytechnics and universities will usually get minimal suport. Despite this, some severely and profoundly deaf students are able to follow courses and gain degrees.

In the USA there are two national centres which specialise in higher education courses for hearing impaired students: Gallaudet University in Washington DC offers degree courses in the humanities, and the National Technical Institute for the Deaf at Rochester Institute of Technology offers science and technology courses. Both centres offer Total Communication as the medium of communication and have lecturers trained to work with hearing impaired students.

We hope that all students will be offered equal chances to take advantage of higher education courses in the future, but there is a very long way to go before this will be possible in Great Britain.

Part II

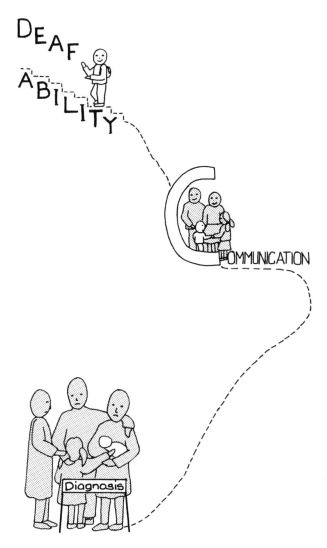

Case Studies

The second section of this book comprises family stories. All these people have gone along the difficult and worrying path that every family treads together. The particular concerns relating to hearing loss are put into the context of family life; practical experiences and common sense go together with the ups and downs of life.

Our aim is to put the first part of this book into context: a hearing test at a hospital fifteen miles away with no transport; a babe in arms and a five-year-old needing collecting from school; the hearing aids being flushed down the loo; going next door for coffee when the teacher of the deaf was coming to visit. Real children, real families and individuals share their side of the story — all aiming for independence, like any other family, but independence through deaf-ability.

In the case studies we wanted to try to include something that every family or individual could relate to their own situation. The choice of families and individuals was difficult and we are indebted to all those who agreed to tell their own stories. The basic aim was to include as many different situations and points of view as possible. Some of the contributors went through the educational system before the advent of post aural or radio aids, before partially hearing units were established or British Sign Language was considered to be viable within the educational system. For a family who have recently been told of hearing loss, Chapter 2 ('Family Reactions') is most immediately relevant — but those stories are just beginning. We wanted at least some where the educational story is complete — warts and all. The thoughts and feelings of deaf adults, their experiences and insights have much to teach us all. The stories range from angry and sad to funny and triumphant; there are strong feelings offered by families and individuals for others to share and learn from. We have sought to emphasise the uniqueness of each situation as well as the similarities which unite them. All the stories underline one thing: deaf-ability rather than disability. The final story included is a particularly good example of deaf-ability — Hilary's own story.

The Kelly Family

The Kelly family live in a small market town. Mr and Mrs Kelly have four children. Their story is one of achievement — preceded by years of struggling with an intelligent hyperactive deaf son who turned the house into a circus with his antics. Mrs Kelly's fight to survive and win through is strewn with hilarious stories — hilarious looking back, that is, for at the time life was far from easy or straightforward. Kevin followed an oral approch, made slow progress, and on leaving school had a low reading age and poor prospects. Now he has successfully completed an advanced craft apprenticeship and won the 'Best Apprentice' in his area for two years running and is learning French and German.

Kevin was the third of four children. He was the smallest at birth. He was hard to feed but by seven months we were going along fine. He was very quick-witted and always one step ahead. I was worried because he didn't make any sounds, he didn't even laugh aloud. I asked my Health Visitor for advice. It was quite simple, she explained, he didn't babble because the other children talked for him. I was coping with three children all under four, I was happy to believe Kevin was alright. He was always a good baby, slept a lot, attractive and content. At ten months I was ill and the doctor came to see me; she watched Kevin playing with the plug and asked why I let him. For months I had tried everything to stop him, but he just ignored me completely; if I actually tapped him and said no he just look amazed — defiant, I thought. The doctor's comment was 'he must be stupid'. I was heartbroken that she could say such a thing about my baby. I felt crushed completely. When I thought about it later, 'if he doesn't understand words he can't be hearing them' — I knew he wasn't stupid. I found a metal tray and loaded it with saucepan lids. I took Kevin into the kitchen, which had a stone floor, then, when he wasn't looking, I dropped the tray behind him. He didn't flinch at all, his first movement was when a lid rolled past him. I took him off to the hospital; a doctor looked in his ears and said they looked fine! They would have to find someone who could actually test his hearing. Eventually at thirteen months he was diagnosed as profoundly deaf.

I didn't know anything about deaf children but it was a relief when he was diagnosed. I tried to be practical and not let it complicate my life, I cried too. A few weeks later all the negative aspects kept coming into my mind, I had to decide to get on with it and think of what we could do. I didn't think about using signs, I simply used natural gesture. We joined the National Deaf Children's Society but we had to travel thirty miles to meetings. *'Talk'* magazine really depressed me, it was full of wonderful children who were well behaved and doing well. What hope had we got? Kevin was like Houdini — he escaped more times than not but he always turned up again. You had to have eyes everywhere. He would never walk anywhere either — no suffragette ever held on to railings like Kevin did. We abandoned local buses because it was such a horror story. He was playing in the dining room one day and I was putting the washing out. Before I could get back into the house he'd locked me out. I looked through the window and he grinned so I asked him to let me in, he said no. Eventually I tried to walk calmly round to the front door — he was there before me and locked that too. It didn't matter where I hid the keys, he mountaineered to get them. Bedtime was awful too. He went up at 7 p.m. with the other children; I remember when he was still in his cot he always arrived down again, he simply did his Tarzan act and he was out. One day I had had enough so I closed the door firmly. I could hear all this noise going on so eventually I decided to go and see what was happening. He had thrown everything out of the cot and was busy ripping up the webbing!

Life was a real handful. Kevin was always doing something he shouldn't be doing and there were the two other children to consider. We had an awful time with his hearing aids. I dug them up from the potato patch more often than I've dug up potatoes! Every time we went for a walk we ended up doing the walk twice, the second time to look for his hearing aids. He hid them anywhere and everywhere he could. It's a problem we never really got round. I realise now he got nothing from them. The peripatetic teacher used to come once a week for an hour, but we ended up just chatting — Kevin would sit there with his eyes clamped shut ignoring us. He was so wilful — how can you communicate with a profoundly deaf child who closes his eyes? I followed the John Tracy Clinic Programme and that was quite a help because it suggested lots of active games. I could involve all the children and they all loved dashing about. Kevin always watched things carefully; if I put my shoes on he was at the front door immediately. He was always good with his hands; when he was in the big pram the sun canopy collapsed — when I looked he had all the bits in the pram with him. He was in the pushchair one day when it suddenly started folding up — he was holding all the screws in his hand. He made life very difficult for the older children, and always spoilt their games.

It was time to think about school. I had met another mother with a deaf daughter, but we couldn't really compare notes because Nicola was so good. It was good to have someone to talk to even so. We hoped they would go to the same school. Things have changed a lot now but at that time he was too deaf to go to the local unit. We all went off to visit the nearest school for the deaf, about fifteen miles away. He would have to board as the school was in a different county and there was no chance of a daily taxi service. There was a lovely new dormitory but I didn't like the Headmaster. I couldn't get on with him at all. We were taken to a room for a hearing test. I was told to sit Kevin on my knee then the doctor went behind me, and without warning she suddenly hit this huge drum; I nearly jumped out of my skin. She really told me off for spoiling her test. I was informed there would be no place available until he was seven. Three more years at home loomed in front of us.

Everyone said Kevin needed school. Then I saw an advert in a Catholic newspaper about a residential school for the deaf run by the Catholic Church. We discussed it with the teacher of the deaf who thought it would be a good idea. We arranged to visit and liked it straight away. All the children seemed so happy, and we were treated like friends. I felt confident that we had found a good place. We tried to explain to Kevin about school, we had photographs, drew pictures but he had no idea what we were doing. I can hardly bear to think about it even now, I question whether we were right. Sending him away broke my heart. My husband was strong and firm — we had to think of all the family and Kevin's future. When he actually went we all cried. I didn't let Kevin see me cry, I put a brave face on and told him it would be lovely, but it was absolutely awful leaving him. I cried all the way home. I sent him notes and little boxes every other day. He stayed a fortnight the first time but that was much too long; after that we collected him weekly. Every Sunday after dinner he disappeared to my mother's house up the road. He would be lying under the sideboard, shoes in the dustbin and hearing aids hidden elsewhere so we couldn't take him back to school. Mary and Liam came home every day from school, how could I explain to a deaf four-year-old that he was deaf and needed special help?

A breakthough came when he was five — it was such a little thing and yet it meant so much. We were in the car, Kevin on my knee looking out, when we saw a big industrial pond and he suddenly said 'Fish no?' I quickly replied 'There are no fish in that water'. I was elated; it was the first time we had had a two-way conversation. It was like a gift for school too when I told them. Slowly his vocabulary increased although his speech wasn't clear. He used fingerspelling to help him. He can sign a bit, he interprets for some deaf friends. He has a natural feel for signs but he doesn't like using them because they single him out as being different. I don't care what I have to do as long as I can communicate. I just wanted to get through to him. A child must be able to tell you something and vice versa. Deaf children do naturally sign; it is so unfair if new parents are faced with professionals arguing about the best method. Conflict is the last thing you need. Parents have to use their common sense and do what they feel is right in their home with their child. I would do anything to stop temper tantrums and get communication going. All our family fingerspell and keep the conversation going.

Slowly life settled in to a routine and he accepted the weekly regime of home and school. Then the local authority said that after his seventh birthday they would only pay for transport to and from school at the beginning and end of each term and at half term. I was furious! I went straight to the Town Hall and explained why we had to go weekly. I made a real fuss and they agreed we could visit fortnightly indefinitely. Residential school placement made it hard for us to be involved, as we couldn't go to meetings during the week. By the time we got there on Fridays most people had gone. Our contact with staff and other parents was minimal.

At the age of thirteen Kevin made up his mind that he did not want to be taken to school and collected anymore. Everyone thought we were mad even considering letting him use public transport; we checked with school and found some children already went by train each week. Kevin would have to travel to the nearest city, change trains to get to another big city, travel across that city then catch a bus to the school. I resigned myself to it, I thought he'd end up in London but I knew from bitter experience that if he was determined there was no point arguing. I used to phone school to make sure he'd got there, he always did. It was nerve-racking but now I'm glad he was so self-reliant.

At the time it was very hard coping with his spirit and determination, but now I can see he needed that to succeed in the end. When he was seven he wanted a bike. Liam had one for his birthday. We knew very well that if we said 'no' he'd just go out and find one, so we got him one and prayed! He pedalled off into town one Saturday, market day, all those people and the traffic! He used his eyes and never came to any harm. One day he had been very naughty I really told him off; he announced he was going to America — fine, go, I told him. He disappeared upstairs to collect a rubber dinghy, a can of coca cola and the picture he'd given me for my birthday. He stomped downstairs and off down the hill — a neighbour was horrified, but I reassured her that he'd be back. Twenty minutes later he reappeared. When I asked him what about his trip to America he explained he was going after he'd watched 'Blue Peter'!

The Church paid for us to go to Lourdes, Kevin, my mother and myself. I'm afraid I didn't come home full of grace. First of all we went to the Grotto; you have to remember there were thousands of people there from all over the world. You cross a little bridge to the Grotto, and I lost Kevin almost straight away; I felt awful, no one would understand him, and because everyone spoke different languages, I couldn't explain he was deaf. I heard all this commotion and there was Kevin with his head firmly stuck between the railings of the bridge. We eventually got back to the hotel exhausted. There was a shop and at that time nodding dogs were very popular; when Kevin had finished every dog was nodding away and the French shop assistant was going crazy. Amongst our other horror stories Kevin managed to paddle in the most elegant fountain at Lourdes, find a tramp who he sat down with in the gutter and was about to share his dinner, and almost set a church on fire when he was insisting he wanted to light a candle and in the fuss knocked over the whole stand. I began to dread every next move as things got more and more out of hand. The poor nuns in the rooms above us spent half their time in the lift because Kevin watched them get in then quickly pressed basement. I wanted to complete the pilgrimage, I wanted us to bathe in the Lourdes baths. I took Kevin to watch each day, and explained that the people going in hoped that Jesus might make them better. I waited until the end of the week and prayed we didn't have the usual pantomime, although it seemd unavoidable, Kevin was very fastidious about baths; first no one had to look at him and secondly he had to have every inch dried the moment he was out of the bath. Well, the whole point was to let the holy water dry on you and it was a public bath. I got ready to go in hardly bearing to think about the fuss to come. Kevin wrapped the towel around himself and got into the water (which was very cold) and simply got out with no fuss at all. That was my miracle; it was a new beginning for me because I could see he wasn't always going to have temper tantrums, there was hope.

At school Kevin had a wonderful woodwork teacher. Kevin proudly came home with a bedside table he had made, when he was only eight; by eleven it was an occasional table. He loved wood and his teacher said he was a natural, that this was something he should be encouraged to follow. When he left school he could still barely read, he was reading basic stuff about pirates at the age of sixteen. He was ashamed of his reading books, I remember him trying to hide them from his little sister. After he left school he went to work for the Community Industry Project run locally. He wasn't very happy, the other lads tormented him at work. It all came to a head one day when he ran off, he walked home along the edge of the M1 motorway because he knew he'd get here eventually. I tried to explain he would have to stand up for himself, that the other lads were simply ignorant. The workshop people were very concerned and suggested Kevin went off to College in the next town on a day release basis. The college had special facilities for deaf students, and other students and staff had some deaf awareness training. People were informed and keen to help. There were other deaf students at the college and one mother invited Kevin home to her house for tea so he could go to the College with her son. He has done six or seven years on the Advanced Craft Course and now he is studying English. The Job Disablement Officer went with Kevin for his job interview; he said afterwards it had been a waste of time, Kevin didn't need anyone with him. He got the job, it wasn't skilled but he felt it was in the right direction. He was offered the only apprenticeship which was going. Kevin was very worried about it at first but he went on to win the Best Apprentice Award for two years running for the whole area.

School wrote him off, said he'd reached his potential, but since he left school he has developed in every way. College opened up a new world for him; they had a library geared for adult interests, rather than those pirates, but with simplified texts. Now he lives in the local library. One of my biggest pleasures was to give him one of the *Doctor at Large* books; I could hear him laughing in bed as he read it, it was the most wonderful sound. He'd discovered books were fun at the age of nineteen. Now he's hoping to tour France and Germany and is having a go at both languages. He always has to do everything at breakneck speed. I can see looking back that Kevin simply wasn't ready for formal teaching, he had no time to sit down at all. Now he has a busy life, he's always out with his friends, off playing football, tennis, or swimming. He helps to organise the Youth Club and Young Deaf Group's outings. Kevin is popular and happy and I think he's turned out a real success.

I have learnt a lot; having a deaf child can be a great improver for you if you let it. I left school at fifteen; for me it has been an education, I have had to meet people from all walks of life and I've learnt from them all. I want to give back to other people now my children are more or less grown up. I helped with the Adult Literacy Scheme, and now I am employed by the local College to teach adult literacy to deaf students. Things came full circle a few weeks ago when Kevin's first peripatetic teacher contacted us to ask if Kevin would take on some woodwork for him. It's good that at last he can do something for people who helped him in the past. We have come a long way from the time I cut Kevin's hair. He was about eight and his hair looked awful, really long. I didn't dare go to the barbers, he had ransacked the place the time before. After a great struggle I managed to cut his hair whilst holding him down. He was furious and shouted 'I'll tell the police about you!' I had bronchitis so I was in bed late the next morning, a Sunday. Mary came running in and told me Kevin had gone — I knew straight away where he'd be. I sent Mary off to the police station and sure enough standing outside was Kevin with a note pinned to his jumper: 'Mummy cruel cut, Kevin Kelly, 41 South Street'. Mary brought him home. If he'd gone into the police station perhaps our story would have had a different twist.

The Munir Family

The Munir family live in a small village. Mr Munir is a social worker in a nearby town and Mrs Munir is a tutor at an Adult Education College. They have four children, all of whom are hearing impaired. The Munir family had to fight to get the children correctly diagnosed and to get aids fitted. Despite late diagnosis, lack of local advice and support all four children now attend the local schools.

Asim, our first child, was late in speaking, but he passed the screening test as a baby so we had no reason to think he couldn't hear. He heard us when we shouted at him from downstairs; he very slowly developed his speech, a few words were quite clear. By the age of four and a half he had odd sentences but communicating was hard. He used to get his hands and pull our faces round to see them. We couldn't imagine why he did this — looking back of course it all seems obvious, doesn't it? By the time Asim was five we had three other children, Amina our daughter and twin boys Mustafa and Raza. Like any other family, four lively children were demanding. Asim suddenly became very ill; it was an awful time, doctors, hospitals, lots of tests. At first muscular dystrophy was queried, but in fact Asim had viral encephalitis. Life was very hard, and at the time things looked grim. It was about six months before he recovered.

During the time he was in hospital his hearing was tested. The doctor asked to see us and asked if we realised that Asim was severely deaf, so deaf that it was a handicap to him. It didn't seem to make sense, after all he came when we shouted to him, and he had some speech; to us 'deaf' meant deaf and dumb, we simply had never met any deaf people. We could not accept he was deaf. Then someone showed us how he had adapted; if he could see the teacher's face he was fine. She covered her mouth so he couldn't lipread and he was lost. Asim was used to the idea as he had experienced deafness for so long, but to us it was a shock. We had no idea what to do. As parents people seemed to assume we would know what to do. I am a social worker and my wife works as a tutor in the Adult Education Service. People seemed to think we would be able to cope, but we needed support, information, advice, the chance to talk things out, to share our thoughts and air our worries — we got nothing. Asim was given a hearing aid but was very resistant; the idea was 'well, he's got a hearing aid, make him wear it'.

We knew another family with a deaf child some distance away so we arranged to visit them. It made things a lot easier. Asim chatted about the hearing aid — was it OK? Would he get in trouble if he broke it? Would it fall off when he played? It seemed to help him sort his feelings out and accept the need for help.

While all this was going on we were worried about our daughter. By the time she was three we were convinced she was deaf. We had trailed round to all the clinics, seen the doctor and expressed our worries. Amina was classed as a very un-cooperative child by the Health Visitor because she responded to the tests sometimes and on other occasions she didn't. At eighteen months we insisted on referral to an ear, nose and throat specialist; he simply said we were over-anxious parents, Amina had congestion in her ears and we were given a six-month course of Actifed to sort it out. The blame for her lack of speech and understanding was firmly put with us; we were bilingual so no wonder our children's language was so poor! We were so anxious for things to be alright that we accepted this explanation and made the decision to use only English with the children. The chance for our children to have a bilingual upbringing was thrown away because of ignorance and indifference on the part of the specialists who were supposed to be helping us. Time went on and things did not improve; Amina became increasingly frustrated, hitting us when she couldn't understand or be understood. Eventually when Amina was five and we had young twin boys she went in for her 'little operation to cure the congestion'; but the problem was that Amina had a sensori-neural loss and no 'little operation' was going to make the slightest difference. Even then with five and a half years wasted it still took three months to get a hearing aid. Amina was deaf, she was six and she had no speech.

It would seem obvious that by now we had every reason to be anxious; both of our older children had severe partial hearing losses and we also had young twins to cope with. There was no support for us at home from anyone. Mustafa and Raza were very chatty, they seemed to understand each other but it was all rubbish to us. Our Health Visitor's suggestions were that we were bilingual, problem number one, and that we had too many children! It would almost be laughable if it wasn't so insulting. We asked the ENT specialist for help, but he simply told us not to worry and to go through our GP. By this time the pattern was familiar — it was our fault, they were hard to test, and by the age of four it was confirmed they had sensori-neural hearing loss and would need to have hearing aids. All this time we had suspected a problem with each child, we had spent our lives with the children having to shout, not being able to communicate easily, asking for help and advice.

Now the children all attend local schools, Asim at the comprehensive and the others at the junior school. There were some difficulties over placement; some teachers thought the children should be in special schools but the local headmaster was very supportive. We had to work it through ourselves. We were not given appropriate advice from the statutory services. Eventually the children were given radio aids and peripatetic support in the local school. There were lots of changes within the peripatetic service, which was a shame. The children all settled well at school, they mixed well and played with all the other children. As a family we have always socialised a lot. The hearing aids caused some teasing and the children had to cope with being called names because they are black. The Headmaster was very co-operative and tackled both issues quickly and with sensitivity, that makes such a difference. Now Asim is coping at the local comprehensive with minimal support, although we are concerned that he's not getting a complete idea of what is going on in lessons. Amina, Mustafa and Raza have a peripatetic teacher between the three of them for one afternoon a week. The boys are sport mad, especially Asim; he's on school teams and loves sport programmes on the TV. Amina loves music; she plays the recorder and enjoys pop music, especially on her own cassettes. The children do give each other help and support. They are questioning why they are different, why they have to wear hearing aids. In some areas different colours of hearing aids are available so they are not so obtrusive, but unfortunately they're not on offer here. I have become increasingly involved in the National Deaf Children's Society and was honoured to be made Vice-Chairman last year. Asim in particular resents this involvement; he is well integrated and feels that my involvement singles the children out as being different from their friends. Amina is the subject of a book called *I am Deaf;* at first she was very apprehensive about what her friends would think but now she is proud of her involvement.

We do feel great anger and sadness about the early years of our children's lives. The first five years in any child's life is so important. Our children would have had more relaxed personalities now if they hadn't had to struggle then. Every aspect of their development could have been enhanced if only their difficulty had been recognised and appropriately tackled. Instead we struggled, we blamed ourselves and we all suffered. We dropped our own language — diagnosis was so late that we felt bilingualism was too much to ask. Now looking back we wish we had given them both languages. They are becoming increasingly interested in their mother tongue and we will be able to build on this. The involvement of an adult deaf person is a good idea; it would help the children to realise that they are always going to be deaf, and of course it would help the children even more if the deaf adult was also Asian. We are sorry about the future because it may well be very hard. There is discrimination against deafness and against colour so we are fighting for their right to be treated equally.

At first we had a lot of anger and frustration to work out but in the end the experience has broadened us. We are more sensitive to the needs of Asian families with deaf children. As a mother of four deaf children I have also become a Tutor on a course in English as a Second Language, and a worker for Asian women. We can identify with and tackle the problems of early diagnosis, access to services and equal opportunity for all. Some parents are unable to control their situation becuase they are isolated and deprived within our society. All parents have some feeling of guilt about their child's deafness, this is not an Asian problem alone. Professionals have to be careful not to stereotype people. All parents must have support and understanding before they are able to make use of the services available; they may need to equip themselves with skills they do not have. Asian and black families may lack confidence, and their experiences of racism are a further problem. In the same way as white families have access to the system, black and Asian families need introducing to other families in the same situation; they need mother tongue speakers with whom they can communicate effectively. People from your own culture who are linguistically and culturally sensitive are ideal in helping families to recognise their problems and to tackle them. We have met some very sensitive and good people and we have the chance to pass on our experiences to other families. It is tragic to think of the many Asian parents who have no dialogue with their children; there is a need to find a common language. Families with no communication are broken families, this is just a problem being stored for the future. There is a much better way forward and we need to develop it.

Justin

Claire and Phil live in a major city where Phil works for a large manufacturing company. They have two sons, Justin and Ben. Justin is profoundly deaf, following an attack of meningitis at twenty-two months. His parents decided, after much heart searching, to opt for sign language. They describe their experiences in trying to re-establish communication with their deafened son. Claire is active in the Meningitis Trust and Phil is a committee member of the local National Deaf Children's Society.

Justin had been off colour during the day and difficult to settle. We wanted some sleep so we took him in with us. At 2 a.m. Phil was woken up by Justin twitching; when he looked Justin was blue, twitching all down one side and his eyes had gone right up into his head. We rushed to the hospital, he was lying in my arms unconscious and I was sure he was going to die. At first it was all played down, but when he was still unconscious the next day they did a lumbar puncture and it was confirmed he had meningitis. Everyone was very positive because he'd been caught early. Three days later he came round. His eyes were open but it was obvious he couldn't see. We knew he might be deaf, as the doctors had said there was a one in ten chance. Nothing mattered except that he was still with us and he would be able to go home with us.

In hospital Justin was very bewildered; nothing made sense to him. I was most worried because he wasn't eating anything. The day before he left hospital he had a hearing test which he failed totally, though at the time we were told not to worry because his lack of reaction might just be because of the hospital situation. We had been sitting for days watching him breathe, praying he wouldn't die, so all we wanted to do was all go home together. Once we went home Justin no longer ran to the phone when it rang or to answer the door. We knew he couldn't hear. He began to adapt very quickly; I was making a drink one evening and he turned my face with his hand so he could see what I was saying. I was amazed. He seemed to accept that he was deaf and to adapt himself to it. Occasionally he was bewildered and quiet, often he was very aggressive.

At that time he had an ear infection and was sent to the hospital for a hearing test. They made earmoulds there, and then said someone would come round with hearing aids. A peripatetic teacher of the deaf and audiologist came round with his aids. Justin took to them straight away. There was no immediate difference in him but as time went on he got used to the change in sounds around him. I was told very firmly that it was essential I did not stop talking to Justin. We had to talk to him all the time or he would forget. He said 'Daddy' first, then his own name, but he couldn't say 'Mummy', he'd forgotten. He called me 'Muna' for a long time. Our first thought was that we'd give him his hearing aid and radio aid and continue to talk to him and he would simply learn what the different sounds were. Eventually the sounds would mean what they meant before.

I thought deafness would mean hard work, but as long as we put in hard work it would be alright. I objected very strongly to the peripatetic teacher coming into my house. We wanted to get as much information as possible but it didn't seem to come. We were just told obvious things — make him wear his aids, keep talking. It was a strange time: three or four weeks before we'd had a little boy, now we had an officially deaf child. People came round and said 'this is a new game, here are the rules, off you go'. We wanted to know about different approaches; very early on we asked if we'd need to learn sign language. Perhaps everyone asks that. We were desperate to do something to help. If we needed to learn signs we'd go along, but we were told there was no need for anything like that becuse he was going to learn to lipread.

His speech did keep going but we started to notice the vowels getting longer so that 'man' became 'maaan'. We were given a radio aid very early on because Justin responded so well to amplification. We had an auditory training unit and he loved it. I used to pop on the earphones and carry the unit round. He wanted to listen to the washing machine so we'd do that, then we'd go outside to listen to a motorbike going past. The radio aid turned out to be quite a problem; I seemed to have wires everywhere, he'd take it off in the bus and children at playgroup would yank at it. It was awful. He preferred the headphones and sitting down listening with me, it was strange really.

During one visit the peripatetic made a video of Justin. I felt as if he wasn't my little boy any more, I didn't know how to communicate with him. I was going round the house saying what everything was — 'look, it's a bike, touch it — look, bike — you say bike, look it's a bike.' Going on the bus was a nightmare; I'd be pointing out of the window at everything, holding Justin up saying, 'look, a car'. He wouldn't look so I'd be holding his head, fighting with the radio aid and saying 'LOOK, A CAR' louder and louder — it was ludicrous. I'd drag him round the shops, trying to act as if nothing was wrong; 'keep doing everything as usual' was ringing in my ears. Everyone kept saying he had to have lots of experiences, I was trying to do all the everyday things and then adding a few extra as well. Looking back I think we should have slowed everything down and given Justin some time. He really needed a rest, not all that pressure. Justin was the one who adapted — we found it a lot harder. He knew he had to see our faces to lipread, we'd forget. Simple things became complicated, just getting dressed for example: I'd be putting his socks on saying 'lift your foot up', but I'd be looking at his foot and not at him. No wonder he was frustrated! Everyone kept saying it must be awful for him — poor Justin. In fact he just carried on and we were the ones who struggled.

After about six months we felt we weren't getting anywhere. We were happy to carry on if we could see progress but we couldn't. He was going backwards. Before he was ill he had just begun to put three words together, he chatted all the time. Now with six months of intensive work, hearing aids, radio aids and the peripatetic teacher he'd only learnt two new words. We were desperate, we asked lots of questions, how could we help; some books were suggested but they never materialised. We heard about Cued Speech and were put in touch with a family who'd used it. We arranged a visit, and our peripatetic teacher seemed quite positive about it so we wrote off for lots of leaflets and tried to find out about courses. By chance I found out that the local school for the deaf was no longer using Cued Speech so there seemed no point, and we were back where we'd started.

I was going out with some of the mothers from Toy Library, a library run weekly for the families of pre-school deaf children. One of the mothers was deaf; I'd never spoken to her really before but we got chatting. I mentioned Cued Speech, and she was quite horrified — *no,* she was so sure that was not what Justin needed. She invited me round for a chat, so off we went again but this time something different happened. Her own deaf daughter, a year older than Justin, was there so they played. They just understood each other. I was amazed, it looked so easy. Kathy got the gerbil out to show Justin — they were all signing and he was fascinated and relaxed. When I got home we had to think again; perhaps sign language did have something to offer Justin. At that time there were some television programmes about sign language so it all added to our interest. The peripatetic teacher was very resistant; she thought it was the wrong approach for Justin. We spent about three months trying to sort out what we were going to do. There were plenty of other things to worry about — Justin was covered in eczema so there was the dermatologist, he had fits so he was sent for a brain scan. He wasn't sleeping at all. Our lives revolved round hospital appointments until I had really had enough. I just wanted to get on with my life and my family. Eventually we went to see a paediatrician; he was wonderful, he played with Justin for ten minutes then simply said — 'you have a normal little deaf boy here — just go and get on with your lives'. It was very important after swimming around in a grey area for so long. We were going to make the decision. We would look at everything, decide what we wanted for our son then put all our energy into it.

For Justin everything has happened since we began signing. If there's a difficult situation now I can explain at least part of it so he understands. If you watch him signing it is completely natural, it just flows from him. A lady on the bus the other 'day said how lovely it was to see Justin and I looking so relaxed together, chatting on the bus. I thought if you could have seen us eighteen months ago you'd have been horrified. He would have been kicking and hitting me because we couldn't communicate at all. Justin's friends have much more idea now; even if they don't know any signs they wave their hands about, Justin thinks it's so funny, it's a point of contact. Now we can get on with the normal things again, learning colours, counting, spelling his name. It's amazing: at one time I thought I'd never be able to teach him anything.

To us the turning point was when we realised that it was communication that was really important. The particular method of communication did not matter; as soon as we were using a method that Justin found easy, that he could relax with, everything became so much easier. You could tell him simple things: Daddy's going to work, Justin's going to the shops later — all the tension drained out of the situation striaght away. You could explain things and he could ask you. It was the dilemma about speech that worried us for a long time; but, speech is only one form of communication, signing is another. At this moment in time speech alone is not enough for Justin, so we are going to use the form of communication we can see he is naturally relaxed and happy with.

We wanted a school where Justin would always feel comfortable, not somewhere he constantly had to fight to make himself understood. I think in a unit, even if there was signing, he would still find it difficult to get involved with 90% of the school. I could envisage him being at the back, struggling along whereas in the school for the deaf he's in an environment where he's happy. I'm happy for him to swim along, I don't want to make his life hard, I don't see why I should. I see him in an environment where he's constantly being pushed along. I've heard a lot about integrating, but I went to a boys' grammar school and no one seemed to think it was important that I mixed with boys from the Secondary Modern — or girls for that matter. Justin has lots of hearing friends at home. I don't think children necessarily have to mix with children from every situation in order to have a good education.

David Hyslop

David is Chairman of the Breakthrough Trust. The aim of the Trust is to actively encourage deaf/hearing integration in all aspects of society. David is profoundly deaf; he had an oral education and is now a strong advocate of Total Communication. He is married with two children and grandchildren. David's enthusiasm for communication and commitment to increasing the levels of integration and self-sufficiency of deaf and additionally handicapped deaf people are immediately obvious to anyone who meets him. He also tells excellent jokes! Here is David's story so far . . .

I was born deaf. There is no history of deafness in my family; I was found to be deaf when I was between two and three years old. We were advised by a family friend to move into Birmingham so I could attend the school for the deaf as a day pupil. The diagnosis of deafness was a disaster for my parents. They had never met a deaf person. It was assumed that there would be no communication between us, that I would grow up deaf and dumb with no future. My brother, who is eight years my senior, was provided with a good education to ensure he would be able to support me if anything happened to my parents.

I went to an oral school for the deaf, taught to lipread and speak; the idea was to enable me to be able to communicate with my family. Inevitably I signed with my friends at school. My parents couldn't sign at all, so in fact we had very little communication. They would make every effort to put on a lavish spread for my friends, but I really wanted the effort put into communicating with my friends, not into the food provided.

My parents faced a hard decision when I was ten, and they were advised to send me to a residential school. It was a strictly oral regime, no signing. I resented being away from home and found life at school hard. Like everybody else I was bullied by the older boys. It all helped to harden me up and to stand on my own two feet. Education at school was twenty-four hours a day; I was taught the basics of the English language and this opened the door to reading. The speech lessons were very taxing, not a good memory. The Headmaster was the greatest man I have ever met, a barrister and natural orator. He made a huge impression on me. He really knew how to talk. He passed on his love of Shakespeare to me, taught me to appreciate the beauty around us, to widen my horizons. I was given a sense of responsibility and identity; books opened up the world to me. My time at this school was a turning point; at four years old I could say one word, at eleven my vocabulary was still very restricted, but by nineteen I was able to appreciate literature and was confident in my own ability. I think residential schools are a good thing — it helps to avoid the overprotection of parents, the cotton wool existence some children face at home. Schools help build character and independence. I had to sort this out with my own family.

When I was twenty-one a group of friends decided to drive to North Africa. This was in 1948, so getting various visas and permits wasn't easy. We were all deaf and agreed not to discuss our plans because obviously we knew our parents would be against the idea. Everything was organised until the last minute when one of the group chickened out and told his parents. I came home to be confronted by my father and my friend's father. Naturally my father was very upset, and forbade me to go. I decided to stick to my guns and said I would go anyway. There was a big row and I left home. We went on the expedition, and despite two breakdowns and ten punctures, it was a successful trip. Our world just opened up, it was a real education and we learnt greatly from our experiences. When we returned to England my parents were very proud and delighted that we could arrange a trip to North Africa. They had thought it was impossible for us to do such a thing.

I was comparatively happy at school; I was getting a lot of attention from the teachers, but when I came home it was back to the silent world. My parents always gave me plenty of love but no communication. I was very isolated and I found it difficult to adapt to the hearing way of life. My parents were middle-class and often invited their friends for dinner, so naturally I had to fit in with their social niceties. I was bored and was starved of information. I wasn't allowed to read a book or join in the conversation. My most used phrases at that time were 'I never knew that' or 'Why didn't you tell me then', not later when the information was irrelevant. For a long time I didn't realise that hearing people have small talk. This was something I didn't understand at all. Hearing people chat; what they say is not necessarily important. I was suspicious of hearing people, as I felt I was missing out on the conversation. I was excluded. At that time suspicion played a large part in my life; now I am older and wiser.

With my brother there was a lot of friction. We couldn't communicate. He resented the fact that my parents were very concerned over me and he never accepted my handicap.

I was brought up in a hearing world therefore I accepted the hearing world, but I also accepted my limitations. I was an outcast in the deaf world. I couldn't mix with other deaf people. I began to go to London to mix with my old schoolfriends; there I signed and fingerspelt with them. My parents were horrified because they paid for an oral education and I was signing. I began to go to a private deaf club and have never looked back. I needed to be with the deaf socially, to relax, but I also needed to be with hearing people for intellectual stimulus.

When I left school I took a job in my father's nursery. I wasn't very happy because there was no stimulation. I couldn't see that there would be any future in it, but it did give me the love of gardening which I still have now. Then I went to work in a metallurgy laboratory as an analyst, but that was hopeless as I am colour blind; I couldn't see the changes on litmus paper. I then went to work in the jewellery trade as a diamond mounter, which was very creative. Communication was the biggest problem. I was brought up orally with good spoken English, but nearly everyone in the jewellery trade had a strong Brummie accent. I just couldn't lipread them at all. I had to learn to lipread a Brummie accent, to be more familiar with the language of the craftsman's world, which is quite different from factory or office language. For the first time in my life I came into contact with swear words, but I didn't know what they meant — so I had to ask my friend to teach me swear words. My mother nearly died of shock when she heard me swear at my brother. My father was secretly pleased as it showed signs of normality but advised me to use it appropriately, in the right place! . . . not at home! His advice helped me to understand the hearing world much better, how to understand the acceptability of different things in different situations, the give and take attitude. It was one of the happiest times of my working life, the craftsmanship was very satisfying. Apart from my job I helped to establish a private deaf club and was involved with deaf drama. After I married I could no longer commute to London, and so I became involved with the deaf locally. I started a Breakthrough group in Birmingham. I strongly believe in the integration of deaf and hearing people.

When I was younger my parents wanted me to marry a hearing girl for the sake of normality. I eventually married a partially hearing girl; my parents looked on it as a compromise although that wasn't the reason I married her.

When we had a deaf daughter my parents were very sad and depressed. My wife's father was partially hearing and her grandmother was deaf so there was a high risk. My wife was upset when our daughter turned out to be deaf, but I started using Total Communication with her; by nine months she could lipread names of parts of the body, and by the age of two she had a vocabulary of more than 500 words. There was a very close relationship between us. When my wife was expecting our second baby my father was horrified at the thought of more deaf children being brought into the world. When Chris was born we knew immediately that he was hearing, but my father didn't believe me. So when the boy was nine months old and sleeping my father shouted his name from upstairs; of course Chris woke up crying. My father was crying too, but with tears of joy. My parents both were equally fond of both of our children and have treated them very well.

We took Judith to the hospital to confirm that she was deaf. She was tested by Irene Ewing — a famous name in deaf education, who said that she was sure Judith would do very well because my wife and I had a good oral education. From my own bitter experience I was determined to bring up my daughter on Total

Communication. At school she had a lot of problems; she was intellectually ahead in her group and was emotionally and mentally advanced, but she was frustrated and bored. I was determined to give her every chance so I actively encouraged her at home. I think I made it worse for the teacher involved, but obviously I was very concerned about her education. I tried to divide time equally between the two children but I think I was closer to Judith whereas my wife was closer to Chris. Chris and Judith have always got on well even though Chris did find it a little hard to sign. Chris was a bit of a loner, he had some friends but didn't want to bring them home, understandably because of the communication problems. Gradually some of his friends understood and began to come round to our house. I had faith that Judith would do well because she had good communication. I was more worried about Chris because he was having to cope with a big class in a big school; he also had a problem of adapting to two worlds.

As time went on more people got involved with Breakthrough. I was offered a grant from the Leverhulme Trust to work for Breakthrough. I was coming to the crossroads of my *whole* life. The Breakthrough job was completely different from my old job; with my old job I had security, whereas if I changed over to Breakthrough my future then would be uncertain with no security. The job would be no longer nine to five. My children at that time were in their teens. In the end, after much consideration, I decided to take the plunge. I am very glad now that I took that chance. It wasn't plain sailing, I had to learn my own limitations. Now working with hearing people has given a great satisfaction, contributing on equal terms to society as a whole, participating in a lot of projects. All this together with teaching communication skills which will, in time, I hope, give deaf people a better opportunity for a fuller and richer life in a hearing world.

It is very noticeable on our holiday projects with hearing and deaf children that the hearing children cope very well, taking responsibility for themselves. Deaf children are often shocked that they have to work and contribute. They find it hard but by the end of the week they have joined in and benefited from the experience.

In some areas, I think integration in units is very good but in some areas, very bad. It depends on the area in which one lives, the attitudes of teachers of the deaf and the principal in charge of the whole thing. The problem often lies not in the formal education in units but in the social life of the children. They are often lonely and find it difficult to mix with their hearing peers. The partially hearing children tend to stick together; this is not a healthy attitude. Some may marry hearing people and join hearing society, and others may go to deaf clubs to catch up the lost years. In schools for the deaf the pupils have a strong bond, an identity, and they usually keep in contact with their friends after leaving school. Many deaf people are sensitive about their intellectual level, of their educational background. There are a lot of barriers between deaf people and in the deaf world. Breakthrough offers a compromise between these two worlds, a chance to mix with both hearing and deaf people equally.

Whether deaf people like it or not, BSL is our first language. We see things visually. Language is all-important: it lets us reason, it frees us, reassures us, gives us confidence. There can be some difficulty with parents who have normal hearing in accepting Total Communication. I can talk from my own experience: you must compromise. I believe in oralism myself, through and through, but I think it must be supported. Total Communication helps to give meaning to language, hearing aids help with speech, fingerspelling to help signing to support lipreading to aid comprehension. I think BSL alone is a mistake, it can create further barriers. Deaf people can appear to be aggressive to anyone unused to sign language; they can be limited because of poor communication, they can appear to be ungrateful to those trying to help, and so can make themelves a race apart. The most important thing is communication: how you communicate doesn't matter as long as the communication is there. There is a rule in my household that everyone is treated equally. It can be a strain but in that way everyone makes an effort to communicate regardless of whether they hear or not.

Communication is the breath of life. Communication helps to build up language, and with language you can stand on your own two feet. Written language and speech have helped me enormously. First it is important to learn how to communicate effectively, then it is very important to encourage reading.

I know that a lot of deaf people would think of me as a puppet in a hearing world but I believe that deaf people should meet half way when demanding their rights. A friend once said that it is no good that the deaf should demand a reduced-cost television licence, they should pay the full cost and demand a better provision for the deaf. I think it is all a question of compromise.

Ann

Ann is at present in the sixth form of a comprehensive school and has turned down the offer of one job in order to continue her studies. Her family are close-knit and supportive of her efforts; hardly surprisingly they are proud of Ann. She has undergone many operations, the first before she was twenty-four hours old. She had been classed as mentally retarded, uncommunicative and the possibility of abuse was raised. The facts that eventually emerged were that she has a severe sensori-neural hearing loss in addition to being physically handicapped. She has successfully completed her GCSE exams, has a practical approach to life and a big smile.

Ann was the first child born at Christmas time that year and the honour of dressing the hospital crib fell to me. At that time Ann was in a different hospital, she had undergone a life-saving operation and I had already spent hours in tears. Ann was a spina bifida baby. I wanted to know everything, some simple and clear facts about the future from the worst that could happen to the best we could hope for our little girl. We started with worst and worked through to the positive; in that way everything she has done above the predictions have been a plus all the way through. When Ann was fifteen months old, we had three children under five.

Ann was a slow starter but we treated her just the same as the rest of the family. She sat at about a year. We attended hospital regularly, but somehow in the system she missed her hearing test. Perhaps the hospital assumed that clinic had done it and vice versa. As time went on I was sure there was a problem. All the children were sitting watching a children's programme and I called that tea was ready. Katy and Matthew came, Anne completely ignored me. I said to Ken that I didn't think Ann could hear; he thought I was fussing. I clapped my hands — nothing happened. I clapped them again, but she didn't move a muscle. Ken told me to mention it to the doctor, simply so that I could put my mind at rest. That was the start of the endless visits to the Hearing Centre for tests. It was hopeless; they couldn't test her, they said she was an uncommunicative child — well, deaf children do tend to be. Ann just stared at everyone, she got so bored with repeating the tests again and again. She was a good lipreader and because she has some useful hearing she did respond on occasions; they couldn't sort it out at all. They said she had a conductive hearing loss and needed grommets in both ears. They helped for a bit but she had so many colds that in the end they decided to try a hearing aid. She had grommets in again at four, by which time she was walking and started to go to the nursery at the hospital. Ann was not communicating at all, but as she came up to five, school placement had to be considered. There was a new educational psychologist who only met Ann once or twice and felt she was mentally retarded. The nursery teacher was furious and completely disagreed. Ken and I were subjected to a very personal and unpleasant interrogation because they explained that non-communicative children are often beaten and abused at home. It really shocked me. They decided Ann needed extra language support and she was placed in a Language Unit attached to an ordinary school. This is what we wanted all along, for her to be with ordinary children in an ordinary school as far as she could cope with.

At home with three young children we had not got the time to treat Ann in any special way. Matthew walked so she did, although I remember wondering how on earth she managed to. She taught herself to lipread so that as long as she could see you she coped very well. At school they got nowhere with Ann using her hearing aid. They had a loop system installed and insisted she wore her hearing aid. The speech therapist was desperate because she got absolutely nowhere with Ann. Eventually the Head put a stop to it all. We all talked and she felt it was obvious Ann had a serious hearing loss, and so arrangements were made to transfer her to a Partially Hearing Unit — Ann was seven and still talking rubbish. Within six months she was talking and learning at last. All that wasted time, seven years gone. She settled well, and the teacher was patient and thorough. We used a home-school diary to keep in touch. It was harder for Ann than the other children because of her physical handicap; by that time she had a caliper, she had had two operations on her shunt and operations on her legs. (A shunt is a tube containing a one-way valve, inserted by a surgeon behind the child's ear to drain fluid from the brain into a main blood vessel.) She accepted her caliper and hearing aid with no problem at all; it was other people who had the problem. Very early on when I was pushing Ann round in her pram people used to cross over the road to avoid us. I think other people's embarrassment is something you have to accept when you have a handicapped child. You can get over the awful traumatic experience yourself, then you have to help other people to accept it too. I think Ann being integrated into a normal school is important. There is nothing crueller than children and Ann has to cope. Locking her away in a special school would have meant she had to cope with all of that when she left school.

Once she was in the junior school she integrated more into the ordinary classes. She had the stability of moving with her friends which helped her enormously. The biggest problem was the changeover of staff in the unit; there were four different teachers in four years, and they all had different styles and approaches. Ann perhaps had less trouble than the others because she always has been adaptable. Despite all the upheaval Ann made progress, she was talking. It was wonderful, talking to us at last. She was in the school nativity play with a speaking part, and she won a prize at school for trying so hard. It was great to see her up there talking in front of three hundred people; I shed a few tears, it was so wonderful.

I think it is amazing the amount of sheer effort and determination she has put in over the years. She deserves far more than she's going to get, she deserves straight A's. We have all tried to help her at home; sometimes I've felt as if I ought to have done a teacher's training course. We muddled along and if we've had real problems, I have rung the Partially Hearing Unit and got it sorted out. We had some very garbled homework tasks so I simply decided there was no point getting frustrated — we would simply leave it, find out what needed to be done the next day then tackle it together.

The comprehensive presented problems simply because the campus was so big. We always want her to join in, and Ann always wants to, but the school would have to understand that she has special needs. We have always been open with the school and they have with us. Comprehensive school was very hard at first; Ann tended to be a loner and the school were very concerned. Her class tutor was excellent, a real support. He steered her in the right direction, and soon she was perfectly happy. When she first began she was exhausted, mentally and physically, but even so she wanted to get her homework done. Home support was very important then. Our problems came with the introduction of GCSE: all that coursework — there was so much it was very hard for her.

She did two lots of work experience, one in a school which she was not very enthusiastic about and one with the local county constabulary. There Ann had to do typing, filing, use the computer, take letters to the Officers' room and so on. She was very happy there. When Ann finished her work placement she had a letter from the Chief Superintendent offering a temporary job of nine months' office work. She obviously did well there. Eventually Ann would like to do that, but she wants to have a year in the sixth form at school first. Ann's favourite subject is French; she was spurred on because she has a smashing teacher.

The teachers at school have always been very helpful and Ann has always been a tryer. We had problems with one of the games teachers who just wouldn't believe that Ann had any problems. She didn't try to understand the spina bifida, she just ignored it totally. The other teachers were realistic and liked Ann because of her attitude. Her parents' evenings at school were a pleasure — a direct contrast to her brother. I totally dread Matthew's reports, he's the clown of the family. When things have been desperate the whole family have waded in to the problem together.

Within her first few days of life Ann nearly died. When she was ten days old she had to have a shunt put in her head because hydrocephalus was building up. Suddenly two years ago we went through a terrible experience. Ann started to have headaches which I mentioned at the hospital; they took her in to do a scan. They said things weren't quite normal — what did they mean? We were passed on to the consultant, who said the pressure within her skull was abnormal and that she would have to be taken in straight away. She would need a lot of tests, and to be wired up to the machine to test the pressure in the brain. The whole experience was traumatic: an overcrowded ward, staff shortages, it was like something out of the First World War. When Ann did come home the specialist said that things were not still right but that they were aware of the hydrocephalus problems and symptoms. We could go back to the ward at any time if we were not happy. He could operate, but Ann would only have a 50/50 chance so that option was out for the moment. We will see how she goes.

All this happened just as Ann started GCSEs. The school have been very aware of what Ann has to contend with and have been a real support to her. All the children need support and help, and we tried to give them all an equal amount of attention as far as we could. Maybe we would have liked to go ski-ing as a family, or go on less beach-oriented holidays, do more walking. We are a family together and we do things together and enjoy it. We have all got different limitations. When it comes down to it the important thing is to treat children like children, not like special cases. Ann has a severe hearing loss and spina bifida but she's also got her French GCSE oral exam tomorrow. Through all the operations and the hospital visits, the radio aids, the caliper and plaster casts Ann has always first and foremost simply been Ann herself.

A Finnish Family
(Profoundly Deaf Parents with Hearing Children)

Both of my parents were profoundly deaf from birth. They had four children, all of whom were hearing. My father came from a deaf family where the mother tongue was Finnish sign language. My mother was the only deaf person in her family, where the mother tongue was Swedish. They both attended oral schools for the deaf, my father learning Finnish and my mother learning Swedish. There was no language barrier when they got married because they had sign language in common. The courtship was more problematic but letters were managed with the help of dictionaries!

I can remember no communication problems with our parents. They tended to talk to us, using sign language to help out whenever necessary. We used a combination of speech and sign to communicate with them. The time when my parents were excluded was when we children spoke amongst ourselves. This could occasionally cause difficulties but we were a very close family and problems were soon sorted out. Now, looking back, I feel that we did not do enough explaining and interpreting for them.

I do not think we suffered in any way because our parents were deaf. In the neighbourhood and at school people knew the situation and were realistic and sympathetic in their approach. I remember when there was a special event at school we all dreaded being asked to interpret for our parents in front of the school. In fact our parents generally avoided putting us in that sort of situation. The one place where we all felt relaxed signing was at the deaf club. My father was very keen on organisations and the

Centre for the Deaf was like a second home. It became an important part of our lives too. We were happy there. We could watch and understand the programmes that were signed, it was fun and exciting. We could contribute and develop our own sign language skills. We knew everybody in the deaf community, about a hundred people, a very big family. At that time in Finland there were very few interpreters so gradually we took on that role.

What became of us when we grew up? My father was very keen that we should either become teachers of the deaf or missioners for the deaf; those were what he considered to be important occupations. We did not all fulfil his hopes. My eldest sister became a teacher, but not of the deaf. She has, however, acted as a voluntary interpreter at many Scandinavian conferences and summer camps. For myself I became an engineer. I compensated for my career choice away from the deaf by being closely involved in organisations for the deaf; I have been chairman of the Finnish Society for the Deaf for twenty-six years. The deaf have always been a very special second world to me; the roots, of course, spread from my childhood. My younger sister became a nurse after working with the deaf. She frequently acts as a voluntary interpreter now. My brother fulfilled my father's hopes; he became a priest and worked for the deaf for thirty years.

I think the most outstanding thing that has left a mark on all our lives was our parents' attitude to those people in society who were most deprived. We had a very small apartment but friends were always welcome. We often had multi-handicapped deaf visitors to share a cup of coffee and some time together. I have clear memories of my father taking me to visit elderly deaf people, alone in Old People's Homes. These experiences and the open hearts of my parents have had an immense effect on our lives. Our house was different from the norm and this difference united us as a family.

Now we have had meetings for the hearing children of deaf parents. We have a common bond which unites us despite our different backgrounds. Finnish society has changed and is changing; the general public are more aware of the deaf and of sign language, particularly through television. There is less prejudice; workers for the deaf, interpreters, text telephones and videos are all available. The deaf still have their own culture and societies for the deaf are still strong, but the deaf and hearing are communicating with each other, building a future for their children.

Sally

Sally is deaf and has four children. Sally's children are the seventh generation of known deaf in her family: deafness is the norm and sign language the first language. Sally's own experiences of being deaf and her account of her own children's deafness, approach to communication, hearing aids and education give a clear message: all children are very different. All Sally's children have attended partially hearing units; the eldest two are now at Mary Hare Grammar School. Sally herself has been teaching sign language and giving sign support to children and teachers at the local school for the deaf.

I went to a school for the deaf. I never liked my body-worn hearing aids. When I was first given post aurals I found it very disorientating. Everything sounded so different — there was a funny sharp sound, it turned out to be birds singing. I never wore my hearing aids outside school. I'd always hoped to be a teacher but when it came to leaving school I came back down to earth. I decided on office work. I was very naive and couldn't wait to leave school: I simply thought — hoorah, no more school, instead freedom, pay packets, work — yippee. Well, it wasn't at all like that. I found myself completely unprepared for coping with office life. There were forty typewriters on the go, computers, telephones, the noise was terrible. It was impossible to use my hearing aids. I also had no idea how to mix with hearing people. It was so stressful trying to keep up with the conversations. I gave up in the end; I preferred to read. Two particular girls in the office went out of their way to include me, to invite me out with them, but somehow I always felt on the edge of things. It was hard to explain to them. My real relaxation was going down to the Deaf Club where I felt at ease, part of things, accepted for what I was. One week I took my two hearing friends with me to the Deaf Club. It was quite a shock to them, for once they found it hard to follow, they were amazed to see me laughing and joking. They felt awkward, it gave them a chance to understand me better, to see another side of deafness.

I spent four not very happy years in the same office then transferred to an office where a deaf friend worked. It didn't last long. I was married, then left to start a family. When Darren was born I watched him jump at sounds around him, loud sounds made him cry. I was sure he could hear. When Darren went to have his hearing check he turned to some sounds. After more tests I was told he had 'lots of useful hearing' — great, I thought, he can hear. When I was called back and the hospital suggested hearing aids I was amazed. Eventually they explained: 'lots of useful hearing' does not mean normally hearing but that he would be helped by a hearing aid. When I thought it all over I couldn't believe I had missed it. He didn't wake up when I vacuumed, he was very visually aware and used his eyes to compensate for his hearing loss. The most upsetting thing for me was that none of my family would believe he was deaf.

[There was some conflict between Sally and the teacher of the deaf who visited. There was pressure for early fitting of hearing aids which Sally's own experience of deafness led her to resist. She wanted to establish communication first, eye contact, sharing, turn-taking. There would be plenty of time for hearing aids in the future. When he was eventually fitted with aids at fourteen months his reaction came as something of a surprise to Sally.]

His face lit up, obviously he could hear. He loved his aids but he loved his earmoulds more. He spent hours chewing them and more hours having new earmoulds made. By the age of two he joined a local nursery class where they had experience of deaf children and the nursery nurse's sister was deaf too. It was a very sympathetic place for him.

[When the next baby arrived on the scene life became much more difficult. Jonathon was fractious and demanding, screaming all day and night. He was initially diagnosed as deaf at four months and by six months his loss was estimated to be in the region of 75–80 dB flat nerve deafness. Again Sally insisted she wanted to establish communication skills before aids were introduced.]

I used signs from the word go with Jonathon; it was funny because his signs were recognisable but his hands were all wrong somehow. I hadn't used signs with Darren so much when he was tiny, the teacher of the deaf objected. When I did use signs with him he picked them up really quickly and put them to use. It was easier with the second, as I had more confidence. We waited until Jonathon was one to fit hearing aids. He hated them altogether, screaming at the mere sight of them as if they hurt him. In fact we were later to discover he suffers from recruitment so loud sounds are actually painful to him.

When Lisa was born, initially I felt she was normally hearing but by six weeks there was a query. At this time Jonathon was

diagnosed as having glue ear. He went in to have grommets
inserted in his ears. It was not a happy experience; he screamed for
most of the time and once back at home clung to me. Lisa was fitted up with hearing aids at nine months, took to them beautifully
and was soon able to say when the aids weren't working properly.
She launched herself off into the thick of things at playgroup whilst
Jonathon still clung to me. After six months of staying with him at
nursery I made the break with some difficulty.

*[The question of schooling for all the children was an impor-
tant one — Sally's own experience was thirteen years at a school for
the deaf.]* For Darren I went along to the school for the deaf. It was
depressing. I looked at the work the children were doing, it all
seemed so basic. Darren knew all of that already; I taught him to
read at home. I felt it was completely the wrong place. Then I went
to visit a partially hearing unit. Once I saw it I knew it was just right
for him. When it came to Jonathon's turn he went off in the taxi
like a statue. His teacher was very understanding and sympathetic
to his needs. Eventually it was all worth it. Now he goes off happily. I think it is important to give the children time to sort things
out — it's a question of waiting and giving them confidence.

At the local nursery people forgot Lisa had a hearing loss. She
signs just like the rest of the family but at school was quick to join
in nursery rhymes and songs. The educational psychologist
suggested Lisa should attend the local school. One word sprung to
my mind — *How?* Eventually I was persuaded and agreed. I did
insist that if there was any drop in the standard of her work Lisa
was to be put in a partially hearing unit. The first year was fine but
by the second year I was being asked to collect her from school
because she felt unwell. By the third year she was learning the
recorder, proud to play in assembly but I still had to go to school
to fetch her halfway through the day more often than seemed
necessary. Eventually she explained her problem. The work at
school was fine, in fact she found it quite easy. Playtime was more
of a problem, and she got headaches with the strain of trying to lipread all the time. She 'coped' so well that people forgot she needed
some allowances made. It was a kind of identity crisis; she wore
hearing aids but didn't go to the unit. Was she deaf or not? Why
couldn't she be in the unit, or go to the school for the deaf? We
tried to explain to her that she really did not need extra help with
her work. It took time, but it worked. Lisa is very settled in the
mainstream now and her work is excellent.

Darren ran into a similar problem — he coped so well that people forgot he was severely deaf. He was in a very good group of children, keen to learn; he became angry and frustrated if he misunderstood. When it came to secondary provision I had quite a row with the senior teacher of the deaf. I wanted Darren to go to Mary Hare Grammar School for the deaf. He put all kinds of problems in my way. Darren would have no local friends — well, that's always a problem with going to a unit, I thought. It went on and on. In the end one meeting was all that was needed; the authority agreed Mary Hare would best suit Darren's educational needs and agreed to pay for him. It was as easy as that after all. Jonathon goes there as well now so both boys have really done well.

[With a fourth baby on the way Sally sought genetic counselling — she was worried that if she had a hearing child that child would feel isolated in a deaf family. Jodie had a severe hearing loss diagnosed when she was four weeks old. A speech trainer with headphones was introduced at home.]

Jodie screamed the place down. We literally fought with earmoulds, and used stickers to tape the hearing aids. It was a continual battle for eighteen months, when she was formally diagnosed as having recruitment. Nursery school was the next battle — be firm — well, I knew Jodie better than that. I was assured that there were big strong gates so she could not escape. Sure enough, two minutes later Jodie had collected her hat and coat and was scaling the gate. After some difficulties she settled but the nursery was very noisy and she had no radio aid. It makes me quite angry to think how she was expected to cope in such a hard environment. Jodie always used more signs than the others and I felt the school for the deaf would be appropriate. The educational psychologist disagreed, she suggested a unit. There was no ideal place so we settled for trying the unit. The first day Jodie wouldn't take off her hat and coat at all. The teacher was very accepting of the whole thing. Now she's very settled and doing well.

One additional problem that the children have in common with me is tinnitus, hearing noises which are not really there. Darren first mentioned hearing scary noises when he was in hospital. When I asked him he said he had often had them before. He had no idea that I suffered from tinnitus too. Recently Jonathon asked what a funny noise was and a hearing friend said there was no noise, so Jonathon must get tinnitus too. Lisa is the other sufferer, so far Jodie seems to be fine.

Very early on when Darren was found to be deaf the teacher started up Toy Library where we could meet other mums, could borrow toys, the children had their aids sorted out and there were formal talks and a chance to chat. At first I used to hate going; it was like starting work again, I could not join in. I did not know what people where chatting about. I felt much closer to the deaf children than I did to any of the parents. In the end it was often me who was advising the parents because I was deaf. Well, that was fine but I needed advice too. Some of the Toy Library groups have been pretty awful but some have been great. I have met some lovely people. The very best time was when there were four deaf mothers and four hearing mothers — a good balance for all.

Sofie

Sofie lives in a small market town in Southern Belgium. At the age of two she contracted meningitis and was left profoundly deaf. Her parents struggled for information, help, a cure. Sofie now attends her local school, where she chats non-stop and is the only deaf child. For her parents the shock of her sudden illness and loss of hearing is still very evident — for Sofie life goes on.

Sofie had meningitis, she was very ill. When she came home from the hospital she was very unsteady, couldn't walk and she was very distant. I can remember clearly that she was sitting on the table; when I asked her if she wanted to go to the toilet she totally ignored me. My husband said she could not hear, but I simply did not believe him. No one said her illness might affect her hearing, and I was very angry that my husband had even suggested she was deaf. Our lives were very tense; Sofie was very difficult and there was a lot of antagonism. When I started to think about it she was always frightened of the noise the kettle made when she was little, now she totally ignored it. We went to see the doctor; he tested her hearing by using a music box. She was completley blank at first then very aggressive. He agreed that she was deaf and that was that. I had no idea what to do or who to ask for help. I spent my time in tears just being sad for what was lost and for not understanding Sofie's problem sooner. By chance my milkman's son has a hearing aid; he told me to go to a town nearby that had a hearing assessment centre. I was expecting to be told all about it, to find what hearing she still had, and how we could help. She showed no reaction at all to the hearing test. I was full of disbelief: so loud and no reaction at all. Worse than that, no information at all either. My health visitor came to see me and asked me why she had been asked to come, which child did I want her to check. It makes me so angry to think how little interest she had, how unimportant it all was to her that my daughter was deaf.

My husband and I decided to get hearing aids as fast as we could. We had already been using simple gestures to help Sofie understand what was going on. At first she just sat and did nothing; then slowly we began little by little to put the family together again. Sofie began attending the Paediatric Assessment Centre in a town fifteen miles away, which meant taking her and collecting her each day. At the centre Sofie has a lot of specialised help with her speech, balance and gym work and so on. She is the only deaf child at the centre. If they had not accepted her there she would have had to go away as a weekly boarder. We could not bear the thought of that. She was already frightened and found it hard to understand; how would she have felt if we had sent her away every week to strangers in a place she did not know?

Sofie's illness and deafness were a terrible shock for the whole family. Her little brother had to cope with all our worries. He had to understand that Sofie needed our time and help but it was very hard for him. Even now when we have a story together I have to look at Sofie so she can lipread; it sounds simple but it does not feel so good if you are the little brother. Our other worry was financial; in Belgium parents are responsible for buying hearing aids, ear-moulds and radio aids, not just the initial costs but all the spares and replacements as well. We pay for speech therapy sessions too. Parents are also responsible for all the transport costs to and from school. We have some concessions, no radio or television tax and no car tax. We also have a special child benefit but this never meets the real costs parents have to face.

We tried everthing we heard about. We went to Austria and Paris to see different specialists about the chance of a cochlear implant. We thought at first it was a chance to 'cure' Sofie's deaf-ness. As we listened and learnt more we began slowly to accept that we were 'grabbing at straws'. Sofie is profoundly deaf and needs the best hearing aids we can buy, and our love. She uses a radio aid now and that has been a big help. After early problems with hearing aids Sofie just accepts them now with no fuss.

As Sofie progressed we had to decide about her schooling. We thought about a local kindergarten but it was very expensive. A customer of mine (I run a shop) told me that children with special needs can go to their local school for two hours a day if the school agrees. We arranged to go and visit and found the school very helpful. It meant that she would be the only deaf child in school. To prepare the other children they were shown a video about deafness; the general reaction was very good. It was all arranged so Sofie has mornings locally and afternoons at the assessment centre. It is a lot of taxi time for me but Sofie is doing well. She doesn't seem to realise she's deaf, she talks non-stop now. In the early days I never thought it would be possible. Her little brother had a lot to cope with, but now he and Sofie talk just like any other brother and sister, they have a good expressive relationship. The rest of the family were much harder. For three years grandparents and other relations simply ignored Sofie and talked to Kevin instead. I was very over-protective too and wouldn't let her try anything; now she copes very well by herself. We have gone from single words and gestures to full sentences and we look at all the positive things, all the things she can do. I think it is impossible to explain deafness, impossible to tell people. I don't look back now, I still cope from day to day but for Sofie it's her way of life and she is happy and enjoying it. In her first year at her local school Sofie had the top marks in her school year. For her the local school was the right choice.

Grandparents

Many grandparents kindly wrote to us to share their experiences and we were fortunate to have a chance to meet Victoria's grandmother. Victoria lives in a village in a rural area; she has a partial hearing loss and attends her local school. Her grandmother gives an insight into the concerns felt by many.

I think the most important thing to remember is that grandparents not only worry about their grandchild, they also worry about their own child. They live through their own child's sorrow, hurt and depression and worry how they will cope with the challenge of a handicapped child. It is very hard to simply listen and give support but I think it is the right thing to do. When I found that my granddaughter was hearing impaired I wanted to find out all about it, what were the options and what opportunities would she have in the future. I couldn't find much in the library so I wrote to Jack Ashley MP, who is deaf and concerned with the rights of the disabled. He sent me some very interesting information. The more you know the more support you can give, but it is very important to support rather than interfere or criticise. Your own children have their own way of coping with difficulties and criticism only makes thing worse.

Victoria was not diagnosed as having a hearing loss until she was four and a half. She passsed two hearing tests at clinic and when she failed to talk after the first test it was suggested she was aphasic. Fortunately her parents became increasingly suspicious about this and at a later date decided to seek an appointment at one of the major assessment centres. There Victoria had every test there was and after a week was diagnosed as partially hearing and prescribed hearing aids.

Many of the problems Victoria's parents have had in coming to terms with the diagnosis stem from a late diagnosis. When Victoria had to go for a hospital X-ray she was very un-cooperative despite explanations and reassurances. Now they realise she simply had no idea what was going on and was terrified. She used to have temper tantrums which made shopping a nightmare and frequently left everyone feeling frustrated. She now enjoys shopping and loves choosing her clothes like any other little girl.

Soon after she was diagnosed, hearing aids appeared and Victoria started at the local school. Six months later she started to become much more confident and to use her voice. I was upset when she was diagnosed because it was something I knew nothing about. It was also a relief because I had suspected that might be the problem. When I am with the family I think about the future, that's my real worry. I was a teacher and I know how easy it is for children to miss what's going on. I know how hard Victoria sometimes finds it even talking one-to-one, so I can't imagine what it must be like in the classroom for her. I see the strain on her parents and their worry. It's different for me. I live some distance away so when I'm not there I do not worry about it. They worry twenty-four hours a day.

Victoria is very happy at school; she has help from a peri-patetic teacher and from a speech therapist. She's very friendly with all the children too. I just feel she could do with more help. The nearest unit is fifteen miles away and has not been recommended as being particularly suitable for Victoria's needs, especially as it is so far away. She accepted her hearing aids; she needed time to adjust to them but now there are no problems. Victoria is a very positive and determined child with a terrific sense of humour. She will try anything and constantly asks questions. All this makes it very easy to help her and to know when she has misunderstood. She's in the Brownies and does ballet, goes swimming and plays badminton. She loves riding her bike — that is where I am over-protective, I always insist she rides on the inside. Her mother just lets her get on with it.

Her speech still needs help to improve but it is easy to follow. Her biggest problem is listening. At school she will listen to a story but she may only hear parts of it so little sense is made of it as a whole concept. My daughter-in-law is a teacher and she finds it difficult to ask about things or bring up problems in case she is seen as being critical. It is often assumed, quite wrongly, that all teachers know about deafness so they often miss out on information. The only contact my daughter-in-law has with informed people is the peripatetic teacher, the professionals involved in the annual medical review, and what she reads in *Talk* magazine (published by the NDCS). Other parents in the same situation would all add their own experiences, mistakes, achievements and make it all seem quite normal and everyday.

Michael

Michael, twenty-two years old, lives in a large city with his mother, father and two sisters. He is a very lively person with an out-going nature. At school he enjoyed most things; his real passion was football, and he played for the Junior League Team. On leaving school he joined a telephone company as an installation engineer. A Mediterranean holiday with friends turned into a nightmare when meningitis left him deaf, and temporarily blind and unable to walk. His parents give an insight into his fight for recovery and the toll it has taken. First, Michael's own account clearly illustrates the importance of attitude and personality in coping with a handicap.

My memories of getting meningitis are quite vivid. I was on holiday in Ibiza with five friends. I remember in the early evening having a bit of a headache, feeling sluggish; I had burnt my back in the sun so we all thought I had sunstroke. I woke up two or three days later in hospital, very stiff but otherwise fine. I don't remember losing my hearing; at first I thought I could hear but I think I was just so full of drugs, I was very relaxed and I was lip-reading. I was also hallucinating — I really thought I was going mad, the room seemed to keep flipping over, I felt as if I was on the wall, then the whole room flipped round. At the time the holiday representative was very reassuring; she told me I just had an infection, a temporary thing.

At first it all seemed funny, we all wrote notes to each other and had a good laugh. I began to make adjustments; I started to imagine sounds, I do that all the time now. When I got back to England I was in hospital and had lots of tests. When they tested my hearing they told me I had no hearing at all and that a hearing aid would be useless, so I've never tried one. I think I gradually lost my hearing. I had time to adjust and so did my friends, they'd been there with me. The big change came when we stopped writing everything down. At first people said something and then wrote it down for me, now I just lipread.

As soon as I got home the social worker for the deaf came to see me. She told me that I would have to decide how I wanted to approach my deafness: did I want to stay in the hearing world or join the deaf world? She advised lipreading classes and told me about signing classes at the local deaf club. The lipreading class was very easy at first. I was top of the class but I got over-confident too. Now I can follow most conversations. I find women much easier to lipread than men because they aren't so embarrassed by my deafness. Men are less relaxed which makes lipreading much harder. When I first went out after being ill it was with a friend from work; everyone used him as an interpreter. They kept saying, 'Ask him about that', but in the end he told them to ask me themselves, that was it. Different accents are hard. You tend to forget about accents but the shapes look so different. I have to think how it would sound, then I'm fine. I see everyone as having my local accent now. When I was up in Liverpool visiting my sister, we went out with my uncle to a pub; it was so strange, everyone in the pub looked as if they had my local accent.

I tried learning sign language, as I think it helps communication all round. At first it was easy but it got much harder. I relied on my lipreading. I was hopeless with anyone from a different signing class or anyone signing on television. You need to be totally immersed in sign, it has to be part of your life. Some deaf people use sign language all the time, it's part of them just like chatting is part of me. I'd never met a deaf person before I went deaf. I just thought it was someone who couldn't hear, like a blind person can't see. I hadn't thought about what not being able to hear would mean to someone's life, how it changed things.

I really miss music, it was a very important part of my life. Now I just feel the vibrations. I get over missing music by watching videos, and remembering the sound. I still go to discos with my friends but the flashing lights make lipreading a problem. Lots of pubs have soft background music and a juke box; I forget my voice control so when the juke box finishes I'm still shouting. Everyone looks at you as if you are mad. I've seen a speech therapist twice and she thinks my voice is fine, no slower or quieter. I think it's because I'm a chatterbox, I've always talked a lot. When I meet new people I just let them talk; if I can't follow what they are saying, then I tell them I'm deaf. At first I always carried a pad and wrote down lots of things. Everyone was very helpful, especially shop assistants. I find not being able to use the phone very frustrating. I write lots of letters now but it's not the same, waiting a week for a reply, you can't have a joke in the same way.

I play football with a different team on Sundays. It's mostly instinct — you can tell when the referee has blown his whistle, no one else is running but me! I find free kicks and throw-ins hard, I never know which the referee has said. The more people that understand the problem the more help you'll get. You need to talk to other people in the same situation, see other ways to cope. I used to install telephone equipment, then I went out teaching people how to use the equipment. When I went back to work everyone was worried if I'd cope — with what? I don't feel so different. They worry that I'll get the messages wrong. I haven't been allowed to drive for the company, they said they couldn't get insurance for me.* Now when I want to go out on a job they have to get a driver for me. I think it's a real waste of company time and money. Now I've been back at work almost a year perhaps it is time I talked to them about it, now I know where I'm up to. The hardest person I've ever met to lipread is my boss, he has a beard. Still, even that is getting easier. I always used to feel drained, but now it's not so bad. I'm a very confident person, love socialising and doing things. I think everything must be ten times harder if you're shy. I don't feel I'm deaf. My advice to anyone would be to carry on as normal, go to people, go out with your friends because they won't come to you. I made a few friends along the way, everyone has helped me a lot. I have teletext for the television, I get the plot from the newspaper first. You can't really lipread because everyone moves around too much. The front door bell is wired into the lights and I have a vibrating alarm clock — that's it!

* Any deaf person who has been refused insurance, purely on the grounds of being deaf, can refer their case to the BDA who will take up the case for them. It is illegal for insurance companies to discriminate in this way.

MICHAEL'S STORY: PARENTS' COMMENTS

When we first brought Michael home from Ibiza we just lived from day to day. He was alive and that's all that mattered. He couldn't do anything. As he got a little better we felt the really important thing was to get him walking again. It was so important to Michael, once he got on his feet I never had any doubts about him. At first he was very lighthearted about his deafness, he brushed it off. Eighteen months later we can see a real difference. He desperately needs to relax, he always looks drained, exhausted. I forget he can't hear but when I saw him talking to you I remembered.

When he went deaf I did a lot of reading about it. I desperately wanted everything to be the same; it never is but I really wanted it to be. I read *Sing a Song of Silence* (J. Rees, 1984), and it helped me a lot. I could really relate to Jessica's mother, the sense of determination to cope and succeed.

I believe in signing; any sort of communication is important, and when that goes a family is really in trouble. I have a nephew who is partially hearing, and who went to the school for the deaf.

He was always isolated, went his own way. He got on well with his family but no one bothered with him. Now I think I appreciate how he felt. Communication is what is important, it doesn't matter how a child communicates as long as he can. Sometimes I imagine that if I call Michael from the kitchen — he'll answer me. I still somehow think his hearing might come back. Now I've talked to lots of parents with deaf children; they all seemed frightened, they don't talk to their children. You must talk to them, communicate with them, it's the only way to make them one of the family. I think Michael thought he would get his hearing back. He lost his sight and couldn't walk, now both of those are fine so why not his hearing? It seems logical. He went to the Neurology department for electrocochleography but they could find no hearing at all.

We know it's important to treat Michael normally, he is almost twenty-two! We do worry, as it's like suddenly having a younger child again. I think of all kinds of ridiculous situations, like train crashes, and I panic — how would he know which way to go if he couldn't hear people shouting? I know it is stupid but I can't help it.

Michael tends to monopolise the conversations; that way he knows what's going on, or else he goes up to his room. I felt if I learnt sign language I would be able to quickly sign what people were saying so he didn't get lost when there was a group of people. It isn't going to work quite like that. We are worried that he's relying on drink to relax. He isn't supposed to drink but he so wants to be one of the lads. Sometimes when he has been to the pub he comes home so depressed. He once said he wished he'd done more before he went deaf, as if he felt he'd never achieve anything now he's deaf. We were told that he was an ideal case for a cochlear implant; it sounded great at first but as soon as we knew it might be dangerous that was it, we weren't interested.

The meningitis affected his balance. At first he was very wobbly, couldn't judge the speed of cars, and we thought he'd get knocked down in the road. Once when we were going to the hospital I was shepherding him across the road, making him look both ways. I fell flat in the middle of the road. I was lying there with a huge hole in my tights and he was standing over me laughing. He always laughed at his problems. When he started playing football again he kept falling over, he just lay there laughing. We laughed with him but inside there were tears. We think he has achieved a lot. There's still a long way to go but he's going to get there.

It's nearly three years since Michael lost his hearing and, looking back now, those early fears and worries have passed. My only worries now are just the normal everyday things every mother worries about and I suppose will for the rest of our lives.

Hilary Sutherland

Hilary is severely deaf. She is married and has two children. Her husband and her younger child are profoundly deaf. Hilary is what is often termed an 'oral success': this success is despite late diagnosis, despite the family receiving virtually no professional help before the age of five, and despite Hilary's wearing an unsuitable hearing aid for most of her school life. Hilary's parents, Mr and Mrs Tooley-Moore, fought many battles in an effort to obtain information and help. Their account focuses primarily on their worries and concerns from the shock of diagnosis to their attempts to obtain advice and information, up until the point where Hilary left secondary education.

Hilary had a number of areas she was keen to write about. As a deaf person she felt well qualified to discuss some of the problems that can arise, and to include some feelings about being deaf. Her major concern was to show that deaf people are people. The simple fact of a severe hearing loss does not restrict anyone from enjoying life, getting a swimming badge, playing for a county team, going on an Outward Bound course or driving a car. Deafness is not a problem for Hilary, it is simply a way of life, the only one she has ever known.

Whilst Hilary is an 'oral success' she has chosen to use Total Communication with her profoundly deaf son. Hilary's husband and children all use Total Communication at home, where it is their natural form of communication. Her parents put their trust in an oral approach: this was the advice they were given, and took. They see Hilary as an excellent example of the oral method and are quite naturally proud of her achievements.

THE PARENTS' STORY

Hilary was the Tooley-Moores' second child. Their elder daughter, Gail, was a lively self-possessed child. She had been late in talking. Her parents remember their surprise when suddenly Gail began to speak, not in single words but in sentences. Similarly, Hilary had shown no inclination to talk and the Tooley-Moores were not unduly concerned. They took it for granted that the pattern was being repeated. As Hilary's second birthday approached there was a slight worry, a need to seek advice. Hilary made no attempt to talk and she was two. She was taken to the naval doctor in the dockyard in Hong Kong, where the family were living. He was a pleasant reassuring man, who saw no reason to worry about the lack of speech and was sure she could hear. When the nurse came into the examination room Hilary immediately spun around to look at her; obviously she was not deaf. The doctor may have had his own worries, but these were not voiced; however, for the Tooley-Moores' peace of mind he suggested referral to an ENT consultant. It was later that the Tooley-Moores realised that Hilary had turned round not because she heard the door but because the light changed.

An appointment was made to see the ENT consultant at the Naval Hospital. There was a hope and belief that this would provide a source of information, advice and help. In fact, it provided none of these. Mr and Mrs Tooley-Moore found nothing encouraging in their visit, nothing to pin their hopes on, no goals to aim for. The consultant was totally pessimistic; Hilary was stone deaf. He had one piece of advice that would provide the answer — children like this are better put in a home. The argument ran that in a home they are well looked after and the family can carry on as if nothing has happened. The Tooley-Moores were filled with a sense of complete despair. Thousands of miles from home, without the support of their family, the only professional advice on coping with Hilary's deafness was negative. The amenable little girl should be out of sight and forgotten, left in a children's home. Mrs Tooley-Moore recalls her feelings at that time: 'I can remember very clearly the absolute devastation. I thought of the simple deaf person who couldn't talk. I saw other little girls chatting together and thought my daughter will never do that. I didn't think she would ever learn to talk. I wrote to tell my parents that Hilary was deaf. My father always said it was the blackest day of his life. It was the day of the Munich air crash and his grand-daughter was deaf. There was no publicity about the deaf then, no pictures of children wearing hearing aids. Deafness was something completely unknown to me, I had never met a deaf person before and my daughter was deaf.' Mr Tooley-Moore also described the diagnosis of deafness as a 'devastating blow': 'The doctor had neither interest in nor experience of deafness. We had never met a deaf adult. The only ideas we had about what deafness might mean came from our parents years before. Deaf simply meant dumb and in both senses of the word — unable to talk and useless.'

The most important thing in the Tooley-Moores' minds was to treat Hilary just like any other little girl. Some adjustments had to be made to allow for the severe hearing loss but normality, Hilary taking her place in the world they knew, was the goal. Something practical had to be done: Hilary would need a hearing aid, the parents wanted advice on how to cope. Would Hilary learn to talk? What could she hear with the help of a hearing aid? What special needs does a deaf child have? In an effort to answer these and other questions the Tooley-Moores began planning. Mrs Tooley-Moore and Hilary would fly home to England. They would visit an ENT consultant to find out just how deaf Hilary was and what could be done to help. A hearing aid could be fitted and Mrs Tooley-Moore would learn how to work it. If possible, mother and daughter would visit a school for the deaf and observe the best approach to educating Hilary. They would then return to the family in Hong Kong and use all they had learnt to cope with the problem that faced them. Mr Tooley-Moore's employer arranged for transport, and Mrs Tooley-Moore and Hilary left for England. They left behind them in Hong Kong Mr Tooley-Moore and Hilary's sister Gail.

Mrs Tooley-Moore was unable to explain any of the arrangements to Hilary. Hilary had no language, no means of communicating; she saw her father and sister waving goodbye in Hong Kong and then clung to her mother. They went from the heat of the stopover in Pakistan to a snow storm in a northern industrial city in England. For the next few months they stayed with Hilary's grandparents. Mrs Tooley-Moore remembers that time as being dominated by waiting weeks to see the ENT surgeon. At last the day came. The specialist's words are clearly etched in Mrs Tooley-Moore's memory: 'She's deaf. What do you want me to do about it?' She had travelled halfway around the world, left her husband

and elder daughter, coped with a shy, confused child for a month and a half to be told that. In despair and disbelief Mrs Tooley-Moore took Hilary to have a hearing aid fitted. Once the hospital had provided a hearing aid the idea seemed to be 'well, that's it, go and get on with it'.

The local school for the deaf were happy for Mrs Tooley-Moore and Hilary to visit. Over the following weeks Hilary's mother sat and watched lessons being taught. She gleaned ideas: the need to speak clearly, explain and re-explain ideas, show objects, give clues, ensure the child has a clear view of the speaker. There was a very heavy emphasis on talking at all times and using the children's residual hearing, however deaf they were. Mother and daughter returned to Hong Kong with a National Health hearing aid, plenty of spares and some ideas from the school for the deaf. Now all the elements had to come together. Hilary had to learn to use her hearing aid, to lipread and, most of all, she had to learn to talk.

Some friends suggested that the John Tracy Clinic in California might be a useful contact. The Clinic provides a correspondence course for the parents of very young deaf children; parents all over the world have used the course. For families who do not have contact with an audiologist or teacher of the deaf it can be a particularly appropriate source of help. Details of Hilary's diagnosis were posted off to California, and in return the Clinic sent lessons. It wasn't always easy to see the revelance of each task but Mrs Tooley-Moore followed the course with care. Comments on progress and problems were returned to the Clinic, more lessons followed. Through all this Hilary was generally helpful, keen to please. She accepted her hearing aid with little fuss. For both parents the hearing aid was their main hope, as this would provide a channel through which they could reach Hilary. They had no speech trainer to help provide better amplification. The Medresco hearing aid was, in fact, of very limited use because of the severe nature of Hilary's hearing loss. But they persevered.

Everyone was encouraged to talk to Hilary, to pour in as much speech as they could. At the age of three Hilary began to attend a private nursery. The nursery had a complete mix of children from a variety of countries and speaking a variety of languages. Hilary seemed fairly happy; she was quiet and reserved but didn't appear to be worried. Her teacher commented on Hilary's isolation from other children but also said she wasn't disruptive or difficult. At the age of five Hilary had one term at the Forces' school with her sister Gail. The Tracy Clinic lessons had been meticulously followed; Hilary had been co-operative, she wore her hearing aid, and everyone tried to talk as much as possible to her. After all this Hilary, at the age of five, had a mere fifty words — something had to be done. The Tooley-Moores sought advice from friends who were teachers. Many letters were sent, the information they received was carefully sifted, all the variables were considered, then the decision was made: the family would return home to England. They would seek a posting in a coastal town which had a good school for the deaf; at this school Hilary would receive specialist help, her language would develop, and she would learn to talk.

At the school for the deaf the Headmaster was enthusiastic and helpful. He was keen that each child should go as far as they could. He wanted to see Hilary's full potential realised. At last the Tooley-Moores were hopeful. They became active in the school's Parent–Teacher Association. Gail was at a local school and with her outward-going nature joined in many activities. Hilary was also encouraged to join in; she went to swimming lessons with Gail. On Saturdays both girls would go to a reading club at the local library. A strong friendship grew up between Hilary and a little girl next door, Jane. There was a natural understanding between the girls; deafness didn't appear to hamper the friendship in any way. Mrs Tooley-Moore recalls: 'I was so pleased when the girls became friends. Jane was so good for Hilary, she always included her. They used to play very long complicated games, really using their imagination. I was amazed when I heard some of their conversations; I couldn't believe they knew so much. The words they used were so complicated. Hilary learnt so much. It was very sad when the family moved away'.

The relationship with the medical profession was not so fruitful. Mr Tooley-Moore recalls a visit to the local hospital to see the ENT consultant. He went hoping for information. The Headmaster had written a progress report for the consultant. 'I went hoping to find out the cause of deafness. I thought perhaps there would be some medical help for Hilary. I wanted to know if her hearing might deteriorate. He had the Headmaster's report on his desk; in our presence he read through it. Without leaving his seat and making no attempt to examine Hilary he said, in effect, she was doing quite well considering. He had no suggestion as to the likely cause of deafness, and he didn't say if anything could be done. I just felt that, as far as the medical profession were concerned, we were beating our heads against a brick wall.'

Hilary was very happy at school, and she made progress. The time passed with relatively little incident. As secondary education loomed into view the situation was not so clear-cut. Whilst the local school for the deaf had provided skilled and dedicated teachers, what of the future? At her present school there would be no 'O' levels, they just taught the basics. The Tooley-Moores felt that by staying there Hilary's future was being restricted, that she would leave school with no qualifications. All the parents' hopes were pinned on Mary Hare Grammar School for the deaf. If Hilary could pass the entrance exam the Tooley-Moores were confident that all their worries would be solved. What if she failed? It was decided that the only other possibility would be for Hilary to attend a private school and receive weekly help from a peripatetic teacher of the deaf. This would be a compromise; both parents and teachers knew this option would not really give Hilary enough support. Hilary sat the entrance exam for Mary Hare. 'Getting in to Mary Hare was everything to us. I was petrified when she had her interview. I think it was more of an ordeal for me than Hilary. We always felt fortunate that she was accepted. When she actually went there she couldn't wait to get rid of us. She was very homesick at first but that only seemed to last for a week. Her time there was very happy. Every effort was made to enhance her potential. We owe a particular debt to Miss Jones who always encouraged Hilary's efforts. The only person who was against it was my mother. She was totally against boarding schools. She thought we had sent Hilary to an institution; she was thoroughly disgusted. It wasn't until Hilary's last year that she visited it.'

Hilary left school with six 'O' levels. She failed English but re-sat the exam and managed to pass. Mother and daughter made an appointment to see the careers officer for help and guidance over their future course of action: the report of this meeting was depressing. 'Seeing the careers officer was disgusting. She was very negative. Hilary wanted to do a course at Art College. We were told that there was no chance of this: she said there was far too much competition from well qualified students. In any case colleges would not accept deaf students. Hilary could type but could not use the phone, and the careers officer felt this ruled out office work. Hilary managed to get a job with the Civil Service.

One day I was listening to the radio when someone mentioned art courses; they particularly stressed that handicapped students were being encouraged to apply. I couldn't believe it; after seeing the careers officer we thought college was out of the question. Hilary applied and immediately got two or three offers. I think the way we were treated by the careers officer was very, very wrong.'

Hilary went on to complete a course successfully. She is now married with two children. Both her parents had one aim — their daughter was going to be 'normal'. She would be able to take part in their world, chatting to friends, to have a job which used her talents, to be happy in a hearing world. Her parents sum up their feelings about Hilary now. 'I must pay tribute to Hilary's sister, Gail. I remember once when Gail was very young she said she wished she didn't have a deaf sister. I explained how lucky she was to be able to hear. In fact, over the years Gail has been an enormous help to Hilary. She always included her, took her out with her friends. It was so important in those years that they talked and helped Hilary to accumulate words. I think anyone who knows my daughter now will agree with me that she has overcome her handicap'. 'I am proud of the efforts Hilary has made to overcome her disadvantage and of the help my wife has always given her. I was a little worried when Hilary decided to marry a deaf man, fearing this would double the chance of deafness in their children. I was delighted when my grandaughter was born without this handicap. Although my grandson is deaf I know that Hilary and her husband will be able to do more for him than we could ever do for her, with greater understanding and support. They are a happy well-knit family and our hopes for their future are high.'

HILARY'S OWN STORY

I wasn't aware that I was deaf at the time or in any way different from other children. I simply accepted the routine as part of my life. I was unaware of my parents' worries or the pressure my sister must have been feeling; life was predictable and I was happy.

I realise now the weight of responsibility which fell on my sister, my dependence on her, which must have been hard for Gail. She was always there when I needed her. I hid behind her and let her do all the talking, she let me join her group of friends. There

is one other important thing which I did not appreciate at the time
— Gail always corrected my speech and insisted that I pronounce
words properly. It seemed hard at the time but I am genuinely
grateful now, it helped me a great deal. At the time I thought she
was enjoying her role as big bossy sister.

My grandparents' visits were special; one reason for this was
that my grandfather had become deaf as he got older. His deafness
resulted in a close bond between us, as he had a natural feel for my
isolation. When everyone else was chatting he would take me to
one side to play dominoes or cards. He loved football and, even
though I definitely do not, I used to go along to matches just to be
with him. He was my only ally when the television was on; generally I couldn't follow the programmes but loved 'Laurel and
Hardy', pure visual humour which the rest of my family hated. I
was able to watch it with my grandad.

It can be very hard for a deaf member of a hearing family. I
vividly remember friends coming round and the long conversations, laughing and joking, the general run of things, the problem
if you are deaf — it was hard trying to follow several people talking, missing the point or only catching one emotive word and
letting your imagination run riot. I remember one day seeing the
word 'hospital'. My mind pictured a horrific accident, major
drama, something memorable happening. When I asked my
mother about it later she simply said 'I can't remember' or 'oh, it
was nothing important'. If I pursued the matter I only ended up
feeling frustrated and left out. Television and radio came into the
same category. My family often listened to the radio; my father is
very good at playing with words so he would make a pun and
everyone would laugh but me. Trying to explain a joke never
works so by the time we had finished everyone wished they hadn't
bothered in the first place. It was a long time before I realised that
timing is important to a joke, or that you can have a 'play on
words'. That was when I felt left out and wished that I was more
part of the family.

I went to a school for the deaf in Plymouth. It catered for
everyone with hearing aids, profoundly deaf and partially hearing.
There was no sense of competition, no criticism of anyone's
speech, simply a bond because we all wore hearing aids and we
were all deaf. There was a great sense of unity and purpose
amongst the parents as well. They got together for fundraising
events; whatever their background everyone helped. Children

who had to travel a long way were often allowed to stay with friends in Plymouth during the week. It saddens me when I look around now, there is something important missing, many parents seem to avoid being involved. They are missing support and help that other parents have to offer, and that they have to give. Maybe being young I saw life through rosy spectacles but that is how I felt at the time.

The big event was preparing for the exams to Mary Hare Grammar School. When I looked back I saw how little I understood of the whole process. Who wouldn't be keen to have all the fuss, a train ride with a friend Michael who was taking the exam too. My mother faced a shock at Mary Hare school. We were waiting and Mum was chatting to Michael's mother; we were sitting literally on our hands trying to chat. In the end we just did what came naturally and signed to each other. Our mothers were astonished. They had no idea we could sign — as far as they were concerned we went to an oral school, where had the signs come from? In any school for the deaf, children will naturally use signs in the playground. I had two separate lives, talking at home and in the classroom and signing in the playground. Signs gave us a sense of belonging, a group identity, something we had in common, not because we were all deaf but because we could all sign.

With the interview and exams behind us life resumed as before. I was amazed by the fuss when I was told that I had passed the exam. I had absolutely no idea what passing meant, how it would affect my life and my family. The new clothes and books were lovely, but suddenly realising I had to stay at the school on my own was a shock. My parents may have tried to explain to me but it certainly did not sink in. Dormitories, uniforms, prefects — it was a whole new world. After the initial feeling of homesickness I settled down and made new friends. I think it was my parents who were more worried. I had plenty to get on with. For the first time in my life I met deaf adults. All of us with hearing parents felt envious of the pupils from deaf families, they seemed to be so worldlywise. They knew about everything, they had been able to communicate freely with their parents and as a result they were more knowledgeable, more mature. There was no language barrier for them to overcome. I realised how safe my little world had been, too safe perhaps. I had a lot of growing up to do, that was obvious. There is a great tendency of hearing parents to protect their deaf children, and it is a mistake. It is much harder suddenly to become independent if you have not been trusted and allowed to make some mistakes along the way.

The accent at Mary Hare was on developing our formal skills but also in having confidence in ourselves and being able to express ourselves and have opinions. I think my parents could see a noticeable change in me when I came home. There were other changes too. I was horrified when I received my first report and saw 'Speech, D−'. I had no idea my speech was so bad. Speech training was a major part of my life at that time; here I certainly lacked confidence, I mumbled quietly away trying to avoid the problems. I had no idea the following sounds existed — *s, t, k,* and *sh,* amongst others. Extra speech lessons were added to my week so I could really concentrate on putting all the speech sounds into my sentence. Well, it must have paid off in the end; I was marked B+ for speech on my final report. I am lucky because I have always found lipreading easy; in my early years, lipreading was the only way I had of trying to understand.

It is not always easy to understand or be understood. When I talked quietly, people complained they couldn't hear me; they seemed happy when I raised my voice, but I felt as if I was shouting. It took a long time to be able to say that I was deaf and ask people to repeat things. I used to nod, smile and hope people would change the subject or go away. As self-doubt slowly melted the situation improved; when it was an important message I asked people to write it down to ensure there was no mistake.

Hearing aids did help me, and there have been vast improvements since I was a child. At that time everyone was issued with one Medresco hearing aid whatever their degree of hearing loss. I happily wore mine until, in the third year at Mary Hare, the Headmaster was horrified to find I was wearing one old hearing aid on a Y cord. I was issued with a powerful commercial aid but it wasn't that easy. The new aid made me feel dizzy and sick, it took a lot of getting used to before I felt happy. The other problem was of being a teenager; the hearing aid was supposed to be strapped to your chest — I don't know any teenaged girl who would be happy about that! We went to considerable lengths to conceal our aids. Often the girls simply tucked a Y cord down their blouse and left the hearing aid in their desk!

We were given some advice about leaving school, but looking back it was inadequate and in some respects misguided. We were constantly reminded that the hearing world was a hard one, that we would have to make every effort to join in, and not expect favours because we were deaf. Deaf Club was not mentioned, making friends with deaf adults was a forbidden subject, something not to consider, a taboo. Careers guidance was minimal. The farewells at school were hard; the bond of trust and friendship was and is very strong, and sixteen years on I still write to most of my friends from school.

After leaving school I had the chance to go on an Outward Bound Course as part of my Duke of Edinburgh's award. This sort of course is challenging for everyone. I loved the rock-climbing and surf canoeing and mixing with hearing people, making new friends. I had an excellent group leader, who made sure that I understood but made no other concessions because I was deaf. Everyone was treated the same, we were all in it together; my deafness was not seen as a barrier, as she made it easy for me to be one of the group. The climax of the course was a three-day expedition in the Snowdonia National Park. We were in groups; I was put in the 'tough' group and given the chance to lead the group for a day. The tent was down at six in the morning, we forded rivers carrying rucksacks and tent, walked through blizzards and fog (despite it being in July) and climbed seemingly endless slopes. The feeling of achievement and satisfaction on completing our course was wonderful, physically exhausted but mentally exhilarated.

Exhausted but on top of the world I left the Outward Bound Course feeling confident, ready to tackle work and make new friends. I felt life would be plain sailing but in fact my confidence slowly drained away; simple things like getting on a bus or asking directions became an ordeal. I wasn't sure people would understand me, that I could make myself understood. It wasn't an easy or particularly happy part of my life.

I had two interviews and eventually decided to work as a tracer for the Civil Service. It was not a good choice. In an attempt to help me everyone overmouthed, exaggerated their speech or shouted. My boss was very nervous, he smoked constantly and spoke very quickly. I frequently ended up with a pile of papers in my hands, smoke in my eyes and no idea of what I was supposed to do. A colleague was very kind in helping me out, he told me what was needed then I could get on. I was always given the simplest tasks so it was very boring, but I was determined to stick at it. I joined the badminton club, the English class and the dance class. I had failed English 'O' level but managed to pass with extra work at my English class. Meeting people was not such an easy task. At the end of a busy day I was exhausted from lipreading, but then my teachers had warned me it would be hard. So — off I went to the pub after badminton with everyone else. I persevered even though following conversations was an awful strain. I was often tempted to stay at home and curl up with a good book but I was frightened of seeming unsociable. Sometimes I was reduced to pretending to understand; it was the easy way out but it doesn't help to make you feel part of a group.

It was at this time that I arranged to meet an old school friend. We had planned to shop but the sheer relief at being able to have a proper conversation with someone meant we sat and chatted all day. Morag was facing all the problems as I was, so it wasn't just me not fitting and finding life hard. The decision was taken to meet weekly, and we discussed the possibility of going to Deaf Club. It was a hard thing for us to decide about; were we giving in to an easy option? My mother was practical in her approach — why not go and see what Deaf Club was like, so we did. Full of apprehension we set out together not knowing anyone there, but once we walked through the doors, it was like meeting old friends. We were welcomed in, it felt relaxed, friendly and natural, and the evening sped by; I couldn't believe we hadn't been there before. There at last I found a chance for a real social life. I joined the net-ball team and other activities. I felt closer to my own family, at ease with myself and more independent. I was beginning to find the confidence to be with hearing people again.

I did a two-year course in Fashion and Textiles at a local college and then found a job with the Post Office as a drawing office assistant. It was ironic, working in a telephone department, when I couldn't use a phone. It was a happy time, and I made a lot of hearing friends. It was at this time that I met my husband-to-be, Jim. We were married and two years later I left to start a family. When my daughter Fiona was born we knew almost immediately she was hearing. When Iain was born it seemed that he could hear; he apparently reacted to all the noises in the hospital but once we were home he seemed different. Our suspicions were confirmed when Fiona caught her finger in Iain's carrycot: she screamed and screamed, but Iain simply slept through it. Iain was referred to the hospital for a special test — brainstem. He did not show any response to the test. I was dumbstruck. It wasn't clear to me that the test only looked at certain frequencies, so when they said 'no response' I thought they meant he was stone deaf. I know how rare it is to have no hearing at all, and I couldn't believe my son was totally deaf. That evening before my husband came home the peripatetic teacher came to visit. It was too soon. I had had no time to let things sink in, to discuss Iain with Jim, just to be a family together to sort out our feelings. When a hearing aid was suggested I flatly refused — if he had no response at all what was the point?

To have happy and secure children — what more could any parents want? Jim and I are no different. My real worry is Fiona; I want to avoid her suffering because we are all deaf. Having experienced the isolation of being the only deaf person in a family myself, now my own daughter has to cope with the reverse. We make every effort to avoid this being a problem. Fiona has coped very well so far, her school have commented how patient and helpful she is. Inevitably, like any brother and sister, she and Iain rely on each other. When they are playing with other children I can see Fiona naturally taking over the role of interpreter for Iain. I have resisted having a telephone because it would be so easy to use Fiona for messages, and I avoid asking or expecting her to interpret for any of us. I think that is a choice for her to make later but it is not a responsibility I want to make her feel. We want her to enjoy her childhood without that pressure. If deaf parents are not careful their hearing children can easily be forced to grow up too fast and give up their childhood.

Diagnosis of deafness meant a lot of attention being focused on Iain: the teacher, doctor, audiologist. Poor Fiona, she had the natural jealousy that a new baby can bring and lots of adults fussing about Iain too. I went to Toy Library, which was a chance to meet other mums with deaf children, but it meant Fiona giving up her morning at playgroup. We managed to arrange for Fiona to go to nursery school, as we wanted her to have attention; after all she is just as special as her brother. I found life very demanding; there was so much advice I began to feel overwhelmed. I always had appointments to go to or someone coming to see me. I felt that every day had to be planned to give Iain lots of experiences. I really enjoyed Fiona when she was a baby but somehow with Iain I didn't have the time; I was constantly being told what I should be doing, nothing could just happen on its own. By the time Iain went to school I was mentally exhausted.

Jim and I talked a great deal about education, about what there was available for deaf children. At home we naturally used Total Communication with Fiona and Iain, they both talk and sign. Over the years we have seen opinions change: strong pure oralism only, the shift towards Total Communication, the opening of partially hearing units and increasing emphasis on integration with hearing children. As Iain has a profound hearing loss we feel he needs signs to support his lipreading and hearing. The first few years of any child's life are of paramount importance, for it is then you lay the foundations for future learning, and we wanted to give Iain the best foundations we could. A partially hearing unit, we felt, would have been too much for him, relying solely on lipreading and listening. Both Jim and I went to schools for the deaf; it is not that we see no problems with that choice, for there are pros and cons to everything. Jim and I were very happy at school, and this is important for any child. So we chose the local school for the deaf for three reasons: (a) the staff are qualified and experienced teachers of the deaf, (b) the school uses a Total Communication approach, (c) Iain would have the company of other deaf children.

At the local playgroup Iain built up a tremendous vocabulary. I stayed with him so we could build on his signs, develop his speech and lipreading and make friends with hearing peers. It sounds ideal but I felt I was under great pressure from the teacher of the deaf at the time. She felt he would do well in a unit, whereas we wanted him to go to a school for the deaf. It was a very difficult and upsetting time. The 1981 Education Act gave me the chance to press for a meeting with the Head of Service and explain our feelings. Yes — the oralist approach worked for me but it doesn't follow that it will work for everyone. Children should be respected as individuals, not shoved through a system just because it is there. We made the right choice. Iain loves his school. The time will come when we may have to rethink our position but we will be ready for that.

People often ask me what it is like being deaf, if I mind that I am deaf. As I have no idea what it is like to be hearing I can't really comment. I have nothing to miss that I am aware of so it doesn't worry me. To become deaf suddenly must be a traumatic experience, but for me deafness is part of me and my way of life. I believe if one of your senses isn't working properly you compensate by using other senses. I know I use my eyes more than many hearing people.

I think my parents faced a much greater challenge than Jim and I faced. They had no experience of deafness, it was an unknown quantity, something to fear. They had no pre-school teacher to help and advise them. Gail had so many responsibilities to take on because of me. I truly value all my family's support and effort — it cannot have been easy. My aim in writing this has been to express what it is like to be deaf, to emphasise that there is no easy way. The most important thing is for parents to be supportive, to understand the deaf child's needs and the needs of the whole family. The method of communication is irrelevant to me; the important thing is to communicate with your child. I am happy with the best of both worlds; we have some great friends, both hearing and deaf.

Appendix 1

List of Useful Addresses and Contacts

Beethoven Trust for Deaf Children
2 Queensmead, St John's Wood, London NW8 6RE
Tel. 071-586-8107 (Founded 1976)
The Beethoven Trust was part of the National Deaf Children's Society, but in August 1981 it became a fully independent registered charity. The Trust is an organisation whose major effort is devoted to raising money to help to provide musical instruments for deaf children.

Breakthrough Trust for Deaf/Hearing Integration
Charles W. Gillett Centre,
Selly Oak Colleges, Bristol Road, Birmingham B29 6LE,
West Midlands
Tel. 021-472-6447 (voice), 021-471-1001 (DCT)
Breakthrough Trust is a charity that seeks to integrate deaf and hearing people by bringing them into contact with each other through a variety of practical projects. Amongst various projects are Total Communication Workshops and Courses, Communication Holidays and Activities Projects. It also provides a children's library, Parent & Toddler and Family groups and self-help for deafened people.

British Deaf Association
Headquarters: 38 Victoria Place, Carlisle.
Tel. 0228-48844
London: 311 Gray's Inn Road, London WC1X 8PT
Tel. 071-278-1005 (Founded 1890)
About one hundred years ago, a small group of people concerned at the prejudice shown against deaf people and widespread public ignorance about their language, founded the British Deaf Association. It aims to protect and advance the interests of deaf people, challenging in particular the suppression of British Sign Language.

Council for the Advancement of Communication with
Deaf People
Pelaw House, School of Education, University of Durham,
Durham.
Tel. 0768-64230 and 0228-48694   (Founded 1980)
CACDP comprises deaf and hearing representatives from
national organisations concerned with deafness. Its purpose is to
improve communication between deaf and hearing people; this
aim is achieved by the development of training and examinations
in communication skills and by administering a register of qualified interpreters.

Friends of the Young Deaf Trust
Friends of the Young Deaf Communication Centre,
East Court Mansion Council Offices, College Lane,
East Grinstead, Sussex RH19 3LT
Tel. 0342-323444   (Founded 1972)
FYD aim to provide opportunities for the young deaf and partially
hearing children to participate in events which are generally only
available to hearing children, to enable deaf and partially hearing
children to develop their potential by increasing their self-confi-
dence, self-esteem and independence.

LASER (Language of Sign as an Educational Resource)
Miranda Pickersgill, c/o Elmete Hall, Elmete Lane,
Leeds, LS8 2LJ
Tel. 0532-656666
Established in the autumn of 1983 to develop the use of Sign Language in education. Three workshops are held annually to share
information, ideas and experience across a broad range. The
aim of the group is to provide a forum for the discussion of issues
critical to the education of deaf children. A list of workshop
publications is available.

The Meningitis Trust
Fern House, Bath Road, Stroud, Glos GL5 3TJ
This aims to provide information and increase public awareness
about meningitis, to support victims and their families and to fund
research into meningitis.

Music and the Deaf
J. P. V. Whittaker, 39 Grasmere Road, Gledholt, Huddersfield,
West Yorkshire HD1 4LH
Tel. 0484-420007
Music and the Deaf provides help and information relating to
music and hearing impaired people; organises concerts and other
events bringing hearing impaired performers together; and gives
the opportunity to try different types of musical instruments.

National Association for Tertiary Education for the Deaf
Ms J. Hipperson, High Peak College of Further Education,
Harpur Hill, Buxton, Derbyshire SK17 9JZ
Tel. 0298-71100.

National Aural Group (NAG)
C. A. Powell, 18 King's Avenue, Marcham, Abingdon,
Oxon OX13 6QA
Tel. 0865-391492
NAG works to promote natural oral language through the
maximum use of residual hearing. An annual summer school is run
for families of hearing impaired children. Practical advice and guidance is available from a variety of specialists. NAG organise
helpline networks for parents and teachers. They have national
and local meetings.

National Centre for Cued Speech
29/30 Watling Street, Canterbury, Kent CT1 2UD
Tel. 0227-450757   (Founded 1978)
The centre provides information about cued speech and also
arranges courses.

National Deaf Children's Society
45 Hereford Road, London W2 5AH
Tel. 071-229-9272/4   (Founded 1944)
The National Deaf Children's Society exists to represent deaf children's interests nationally and locally, and to support parents
through a large network of self-help groups. It is a voluntary
organisation, the activities of which are co-ordinated from a small
head office. They provide a wealth of advice, information and
support on a wide range of subjects relating to hearing impaired
children.

National Deaf Children's Society Technology Information Centre
4 Church Road, Edgbaston, Birmingham B15 3TD
Tel. 021-454-5151 (voice), 021-454-9795 (Vistel)
NDCS Technology Information Centre provides up-to-date information on hearing aids, radio aids and other aids that may help deaf children.

Paget Gorman Society
3 Gypsy Lane, Headington, Oxford OX3 7PT
Tel. 0865-61908   (Founded 1951)
The Society provides information and advice on PGSS for parents and professionals. It also acts as an examining body and awards certificates and diplomas to those who qualify for them.

Royal National Institute for the Deaf
105 Gower Street, London WC1E 6AH
Tel. 071-387-8033   (Founded 1911)
RNID is a voluntary organisation representing the interests of deaf, deaf-blind and hard of hearing people. It ensures that their needs are properly recognised by both the government and the general public and that facilities and services for deaf people are continually improved.

SENSE
(National Association for Deaf-Blind and Rubella Handicapped)
311 Gray's Inn Road, London WC1X 8PT
Tel. 071-278-1005   (Founded 1955)
SENSE offer help and advice to deaf-blind children and adults, to their families and to people who work with them.

John Tracy Clinic
807 W. Adams Blvd, Los Angeles, California 90007, USA
The John Tracy Clinic was set up in the 1940s. It has been used by a wide variety of parents all over the world. It is particularly useful for parents who do not have access to counselling from teachers of the deaf or audiologists. The clinic runs a correspondence course for parents of deaf children. Parents send details and receive a step-by-step schedule to follow. Families have to be prepared to follow carefully.

Working Party on Signed English
Miss M. Kennedy, Heathlands School for Deaf Children,
Heathlands Drive, St Albans, Hertfordshire AL3 5AM
Tel. 0727-68596/63950

Appendix 2

Hearing Aid Management

Daily Checks

Work through each stage, checking that:

1. The batteries are working: when the aid is switched on to full volume it should produce a loud whistle. If necessary replace the batteries.
2. There are no signs of physical damage, cracked casing, teeth marks; that the microphone is intact. In the case of body-worn aids the microphone grill should be free of sand, dinner, playdough, etc.
3. The mould is clean and unblocked; a pipecleaner may be helpful in removing stubborn wax.
4. The aid should then be attached to a stetoclip — this allows parents and teachers to listen to the child's aid. Be careful to ensure the volume control is adjusted to a low setting. Simply talk to yourself and listen to the aid via the stetoclip; the sound will be metallic in quality, but should be clear and free from distortion. If you listen to your child's aid routinely you will soon learn to pick out problems.

Troubleshooting

Problem: No sound from the hearing aid when it is switched on

	Post Aural	Body-worn
Switch aid on — not to 'T'	√	√
Replace battery: ensure in correctly	√	√
Mould unblocked	√	√
Replace hook	√	
Ensure tubing is not twisted	√	
Replace lead		√
Replace receiver		√

Check each possibility one by one until you isolate the fault. Remember that an aid may have more than one fault.

Loose components can be identified by gently shaking the aid and listening for the rattle as they slide around. Return the aid to your hearing aid centre in this case.

If you can cause the aid to go on and off by gently squeezing the casing then the aid is intermittent. Return it to your hearing aid centre for repair.

By routinely checking your child's aids, identifying simple problems and dealing with them, you ensure your child has an effective hearing aid and help to keep the system running.

Earmoulds

Problem: Loud whistling when your child is wearing his hearing aid

a. The most common cause of feedback whistling is badly fitting moulds. In this case arrange for new moulds to be made.
b. Ensure the earmould is correctly inserted in your child's ear. If you are unsure how to do this ask your teacher of the deaf or audiologist to show you.
c. Post aural aids: the hook may be chewed or loose. Check for damage and tighten onto hearing aid. Check the tubing is firmly attached to hook and is not cracked. Replace if necessary.
d. Body-worn aids: The receiver should fit tightly into the lockspring in the earmould. Replace if necessary. Children should be issued with miniature receivers. This avoids the weight of the receiver levering the earmould out of the child's ear.
e. Ensure the mould itself is not cracked or split. Arrange for new earmould if necessary.
f. Remember that hard wax in the ear canal or a middle ear infection can cause feedback.

EARMOULDS: POINTS TO REMEMBER

1. Earmoulds need replacing regularly as your child grows. You will know when new earmoulds are needed as the aid will whistle when you try to put it to the correct setting.

2. Earmoulds should be washed in warm soapy water regularly. Remember to remove the hearing aid before you wash the earmould. An old toothbrush is useful for scrubbing round earmoulds. Dry it, ensuring that there is no water left in the tubing, before you re-attach it to the hearing aid. It may be helpful to do this each evening, giving the mould a chance to dry out before the morning.

3. Any droplets of water which collect in the tubing, as your child runs around, must be removed. The droplets greatly reduce the efficiency of hearing aids. Small blowers are available for this purpose; ask your teacher of the deaf or audiologist.

4. Ensure that the earmould is attached correctly to a post aural aid. The curve of the earmould fits inside the curve of the hearing aid.

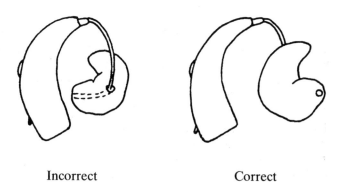

Incorrect   Correct

5. Ensure the mould is fitted correctly into the ear.

6. Post aural aids have tubing connecting the aid to the earmould — this tubing needs to be supple. Your teacher of the deaf or audiologist will be able to show you how to re-tube earmoulds.

7. The hook which attaches the tubing to the hearing aid in post aural aids should fit tightly on to the aid. Children frequently chew hooks; bent, collapsed and discoloured hooks need replacing. There are many types of hooks: check that any replacements are correct for your child's aid.

Care of Radio Hearing Aids: Fault Finding

There are a variety of radio aid systems in use. Parents should ask their audiologist for advice on daily use including routine checks; it is most helpful if you have this information written down to refer to. Some manufacturers provide helpful instruction leaflets; ask whether one is available. Ensure that batteries and battery packs are fully charged before you use or check a radio aid.

Type 1 Radio Aid: used as a conventional hearing aid and radio aid. This type of aid is in two parts: (i) transmitter, (ii) receiver which also acts as a hearing aid. Check both aspects of this type of radio aid, (a) conventional hearing aid facility, (b) radio aid facility.

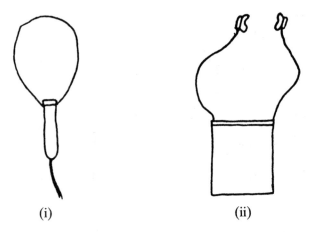

          (i)   (ii)

a. (i) Check *transmitter* for damage and debris, particularly the microphone. Check the aerial is intact. Remove any accumulated debris with a soft cloth.

  (ii) Check the *receiver*. The radio facility should be switched off. The aid is then checked as an ordinary body-worn aid: batteries, listening through a stetoclip, check leads and receivers. Ensure the sound is not intermittent or distorted by wiggling the lead. Check that the microphone grills are clean.

b. (i) The crystal oscillator should be in place in the child's receiver. The radio facility should be switched on. Ensure that the environmental microphones are switched off.

(ii) Switch the transmitter on and, by using a helper, radio, television or other sound source in an adjacent room, listen to
the sound through the stetoclip. Ensure it is clear, good
quality sound. Check each lead separately.

The most common problem is faulty batteries (inadequately
charged, incorrectly inserted), poor contacts or a faulty charger. If
you have been given replacement leads and receivers these can be
used to isolate the problem area. If you have tried all the possibilities and can get no response, seek professional help.

Type 2 Radio Aid: Radio aid used with conventional hearing
aids, post aural or body-worn.

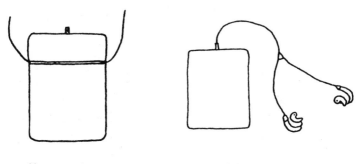

(i) transmitter   (ii) receiver

1. Check that the conventional hearing aids are working properly
using a stetoclip.
2. Ensure that the transmitter and receiver have fully charged,
correctly fitted batteries.
3. Switch on the transmitter and receiver. Attach a radio aid 'listening stick' to the receiver. Place the transmitter in an adjacent
room near a sound source. Return to the receiver and listen to
it through the listening stick. If there is no sound, check:
    (i)   the transmitter and receiver are both switched on, and that
          they are on the same frequency.
    (ii) the transmitter aerial is intact.
    (iii) replace the batteries to ensure this is not the problem.
    (iv) if you have a replacement microphone, change the trans-
          mitter microphone and its lead, if in use.

If, after all these checks, there is still no sound, contact your teacher of the deaf or audiologist.

4. If the radio system is working, attach the hearing aid to your child's radio aid. Repeat the check (3) listening through a stetoclip attached to the conventional hearing aids. Ensure your child's aid is switched on to the appropriate setting to receive radio transmission (aids vary so you will need to check this with your teacher of the deaf or audiologist). If there is no sound, check:

   (i)   the lead: remove, replace and listen again.

   (ii) the input shoe is not damaged; replace if necessary and check.

   (iii) some post aural aids have a small audio connector on the side, like this
   Ensure it is clean and intact. This occasionally becomes covered by micropore tape, stickies and the like.

   (iv) the direct input lead is intact, and the pins have not been bent or snapped off. If this type of lead continually falls out ask for a replacement aid. The springs in the input socket will need replacing.

If there is still no sound the aid is faulty and needs to be returned to your teacher of the deaf or audiologist.

Auxiliary Aids for the Hearing Impaired

There are a number of environmental aids available on the market, the type and quality of which are changing all the time. For parents in Great Britain there is an excellent resource centre in Birmingham run by the National Deaf Children's Society; the centre offers unbiased and up-to-date information on technical aids for use with hearing impaired children. The centre also lends out radio aids to families on a trial basis, and may be able to offer some financial help to parents who want to purchase a radio aid. There is an exhibition and display area where parents can have a close look at equipment. Expert information and advice is offered, together with practical demonstrations of equipment. The Technology Centre in Birmingham is open to the public, but it is advisable to make prior arrangements. The Centre also holds open days and welcomes groups of parents and professionals.

For further information, please contact The National Deaf Children's Society, Technology Information Centre, 4 Church Road, Edgbaston, Birmingham B15 3TD (Tel. 021-454-5151 (voice), 021-454-9795 (Vistel); Freefone 0800 424545 1.00 p.m. to 5.00 p.m., for parents only).

In addition to listing some equipment that is available the addresses of various manufacturers are included (see book list). Prices may vary, and it is worth seeking local advice before purchasing specialised goods. Ask if there is an Environmental Aids officer in your area. She may be based at the local Centre for the Deaf or at the Department of Social Services. Your local education service or branch of the NDCS may have equipment you can borrow in order to assess its value. Some companies do not charge Value Added Tax (VAT) on equipment bought for children with special needs; enquire whether a VAT exemption certificate is available from the manufacturer. Teletext televisions and telephones are not exempt from VAT, as they can be used by hearing as well as hearing impaired people.

SOME OF THE AIDS WHICH MIGHT BE HELPFUL FOR DEAF CHILDREN

Teddy Bear with flashing lights

The teddy bear's eyes light up when anyone uses their voice nearby. A child babbling or talking to the teddy is 'rewarded' by seeing teddy's eyes flash back.

Hello Ted

Speech Apple
Another toy to encourage children to use their voices. In this case a worm creeps out of the apple: the louder the voice the more the worm glows.

Loopy Ted

Loopy Ted is a form of induction loop that can be attached to a tape recorder, television or radio. The child's aid must be switched to the 'T' position. The loop device is inside the teddy's head so the nearer the child's hearing aid is to the teddy the better the signal. The manufacturer recommends Loopy Ted for children with losses no greater than 90–100 dB.

Sound Activated Monkey

The idea behind this is to encourage children to practise their pronunciation of 'S'. The toy monkey is attached to the unit and when 'S' reaches the detection level, the monkey climbs the pole.

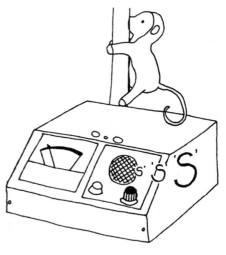

There are a vast number of noise-making and noise-activated toys on the market. Check what is available and proved to be useful with your teacher of the deaf, Toy Library, drop-in centre and other parents. If you can borrow toys to try them out do so as this not only saves money but also avoids frustration and disappointment.

ENVIRONMENTAL AIDS FOR HOME USE

Doorbell Alarm

This is worked from a normal bell push button. When the doorbell rings, the lights can flash on and off through the existing mains wiring. There is another model which doesn't need to be connected to the wiring system; it runs on batteries and is portable. This is ideal for a small bedsit or a flat.

Alarm Clock

The Flashing Alarm Clock is a clock attached to a bedside lamp: when the alarm clock rings the lamp flashes the light on and off. The unit will carry on flashing until the person is woken up to switch the alarm off.

For heavy sleepers the vibrating alarm clock is better. When the alarm goes off the vibrator pad vibrates under the pillow until the alarm is switched off.

Smoke Detection Alarm

An early warning fire alarm system; it can be connected to the lights, to the vibrating system or to both.

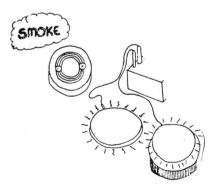

Baby Alarm

A microphone is sited
near the baby and the
wire is connected to the
lamp: when the baby
cries the lamp flashes.
This alarm can also be
used as a telephone or
doorbell indicator.

Amplified Handset

This involves a telephone
handset with a volume control
which is set in the side of the
earpiece. You can get a portable
version which fits all types of
phones. An inductive coupler
can help to clarify the speech but
the user must have a 'T' switch
on their hearing aid. The
various telephone aids will not
be suitable for all those who
have hearing losses; discuss the
possibilities with an Environmental Aids Officer. Some
telephones have a built-in loop.

Minicom or Vistel

An ordinary phone can be
attached to Minicom or Vistel.
The caller's message is typed
into the machine and is
transmitted along the telephone
wire to appear on a display
screen on the receiving
machine.

Television Adaptor

This can allow the listener to
listen through the earpiece
directly to the television with
control over the sound level
which will not affect other
people listening at the same
time. There are a wide variety
of television adaptors; consult
your Environmental Aids
Officer for advice.

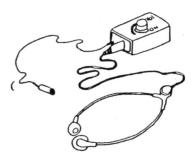

Loop System

A wire is placed around the
room. The hearing aid user
must sit within the cable so that
when the aid is switched to 'T'
position it can pick up the
sound signal from the television
with no background inter-
ference. There are also other
kinds of loops. When you see
the 'T' symbol in public
buildings it means that there is
a loop system in that building,
e.g. in banks and Post Offices.

Teletext Adaptor

A teletext adaptor can
allow a non-teletext
television set to receive
Ceefax and Oracle
subtitles on their
programmes. It can also
record any subtitled
programmes on a video
recorder.

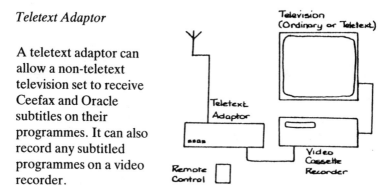

Booklist

Diagnosis and Medical Aspects

BALLANTYNE, J. and MARTIN, J. A. (1984) *Deafness*. Churchill Livingstone.

COWAN, D. L. (1986) *Coping with Ear Problems*. Chambers.

FREEMAN, R., CARBIN, C. F. and BOESE, R. (1981) *Can't Your Child Hear? A Guide for Those Who Care about Deaf Children*. Baltimore: University Park Press.

McCORMICK, B. (1988) *Screening for Hearing Impairment in Young Children*. Croom Helm.

MARTIN, M. and GROVER, B. (1986) *Hearing Loss*. Churchill Livingstone.

TUCKER, I. and NOLAN, M. (1984) *Educational Audiology*. Croom Helm.

Deafness and the Family

FREEMAN, P. (1975) *Understanding the Deaf/Blind Child*. Heinemann.

GREEN, C. (1984) *Toddler Taming — A Parents' Guide to the First Four Years*. Century Press.

GREGORY, S. (1981) *The Deaf Child and His Family*. Souvenir Press.

LUTERMAN, D. (1967) *Deafness in the Family*. College-Hill Press.

MEADOW, K. P. (1980) *Deafness and Child Development*. Edward Arnold.

NOLAN, M. and TUCKER, I. (1988) *The Hearing Impaired Child and the Family*. Souvenir Press.

OGDEN, P. and LIPSETT, S. (1982) *The Silent Garden: Understanding the Hearing Impaired Child*. St. Martin's Press.

SHERIDAN, M. (1975) *From Birth to Five Years*. NFER/Nelson.

WYMAN, R. (1986) *Multiply Handicapped Children*. Souvenir Press.

Hearing Aids

MARTIN, M. and GROVER, B. (1986) *Hearing Loss*. Churchill Livingstone.

ROSS, M. (1972) Hearing aid selection for pre-verbal hearing impaired children. In M. POLLACK (ed.) *Amplification for the Hearing Impaired.* Grune and Stratton.

ROSS, M. (1977) Hearing aids. In B. F. JAFFEE (ed.) *Hearing Loss in Children,* pp. 676–98. University Park Press.

TUCKER, I. and NOLAN, M. (1984) *Educational Audiology.* Croom Helm.

Language Development

CALVERT, D. R. and SILVERMAN, S. R. (1975) *Speech and Deafness: A Text for Learning and Teaching.* Alexander Graham Bell Association for the Deaf.

CRYSTAL, D. (1976) *Child Language, Learning and Linguistics.* Edward Arnold.

CRYSTAL, D. (1986) *Listen to Your Child.* Penguin.

De VILLIERS, P. and De VILLIERS, J. (1979) *Early Language.* Fontana Paperbacks.

LEWIS, D. (1978) *The Secret Language of Your Child: How Children Learn to Talk before They can Speak.* Souvenir Press.

LING, D. (1976) *Speech and the Hearing Impaired Child: Theory and Practice.* Alexander Graham Bell Association for the Deaf.

McCONKEY, R. and PRICE, P. (1986) *Let's Talk: Learning Language in Everyday Settings.* Human Horizons Series. Souvenir Press.

PLAYMATTERS (1988) Hear and say: toys for children with hearing, speech and language difficulties. Available from Playmatters, 68 Churchway, London NW1 1LT.

VAN UDEN, A. (1977) *A World of Language for Deaf Children,* Part 1: *Basic Principles.* Swets and Zeitlinger.

WOOD, D., WOOD, H., GRIFFITHS, A. and HOWARTH, I. (1986) *Teaching and Talking with Deaf Children.* J. Wiley and Sons.

Sign Language

BAKER, C. and BATTISON, R. (eds) (1980) *Sign Language and the Deaf Community.* Silver Springs, MD: NAD.

COMMUNICATION LINK (1985) *A Dictionary of Signs.* Beverley School for the Deaf, Beverley Road, Saltersgill, Middlesborough, Cleveland. (BSL.)

COMMUNICATION LINK (1986) *Songs in Sign for Children.* Beverley School for the Deaf, Beverley Road, Saltersgill, Middlesborough, Cleveland. (BSL.)

HOUGH, J. (1983) *Louder than Words.* Great Ouse Press.

KYLE, J., WOLL, B., PULLEN, G. and MADDIX, F. (1985) *Sign Language: The Study of Deaf People and Their Language.* Cambridge University Press.

LANE, H. (1988) *When the Mind Hears: A History of the Deaf.* Penguin.

MILES, D. (1988) *British Sign Language: A Beginner's Guide.* BBC. A video is available to accompany this book, from BBC Enterprises.

RNID (1976) *Methods of Communication Currently Used in the Education of Deaf Children.* RNID.

SCHLESINGER, H. and MEADOW, K. (1974) *Sound and Sign: Childhood Deafness and Mental Health.* University of California.

WOLL, B., KYLE, J. and DEUCHAR, M. (1981) *Perspectives on British Sign Language and Deafness.* Croom Helm.

Educational Aspects

BRILL, R. G. (1978) *Mainstreaming the Pre-lingually Deaf Child.* Gallaudet College Press.

CONRAD, R. (1979) *The Deaf School Child.* Harper and Row.

LYNAS, W. (1986) *Integrating the Handicapped into Ordinary Schools — A Study of Hearing-impaired Pupils.* Croom Helm.

QUIGLEY, S. P. and KRETSCHMER, R. E. (1982) *The Education of Deaf Children.* Edward Arnold.

REED, M. (1984) *Educating Hearing Impaired Children in Ordinary and Special Schools.* Open University Press.

SOMERSET EDUCATION AUTHORITY (1981) *Ways and Means, 3: Hearing.* Globe Educational.

TURNER, G. (1983) *The Right Job for You: Careers Guidance for the Hearing Impaired.* Heinemann Medical Books Ltd.

WEBSTER, A. and ELLWOOD, J. (1985) *The Hearing Impaired Child in the Ordinary School.* Croom Helm.

Music

KEINER, R. (1984) *Music for Deaf Children — A Practical Guide for Parents and Teachers.* Available from Mrs Keiner, 14 Goldsmith Road, London W3 6PX.

ROBBINS, C. and ROBBINS, C. (1980) *Music for the Hearing Impaired.* Magna-Music Baton Inc. Available in UK from H. and T. Clement, Broome Farm Village Stores, 2 Cottage Farm, Broome, Clent, Nr Stourbridge, Worcs. DY9 0HA.

ROBERTS, S. (1987) *Playsongs.* Available from Playsongs, 39 Byne Road, Sydenham, London SE26 5JF. (A practical book for parents including tape cassette, with ideas for all the family to join in and enjoy music.)

TAIT, M. (1985) *Reaching our Children through Song: An Approach to the Development of Communication with Deaf Pre-Schoolers.* Available from Psychology Dept, University of Nottingham, Nottingham.

A comprehensive list of publications relating to music and the hearing impaired is produced by the Music Advisory Service, Disabled Living Foundation, 380–384 Harrow Road, London W9 2HU.

Biographies

ASHLEY, J. (1973) *A Journey into Silence.* Bodley Head.

BROOK, M. (1984) *Christopher — A Silent Life.* Bedford Press/ NCVO for SENSE — the National Deaf-Blind and Rubella Association.

FLETCHER, L. (1987) *A Language for Ben.* Souvenir Press.

PETTENUZZO, B. and MUNIR, A. (1987) *I am Deaf — Brenda Pettenuzzo meets Amina Munir.* Franklin Watts.

REES, J. (1984) *Sing a Song of Silence: A Deaf Girl's Odyssey.* Futura.

ROBINSON, K. (1987) *Children of Silence — The Story of Sarah and Joanne.* Gollancz.

WALKER, L. A. (1987) *A Loss for Words.* Fontana.

WRIGHT, D. (1969) *Deafness: A Personal Account.* Allen Lane/ Penguin.

Children's Books with Sign Language 'Text'

DEAF ADVISORY SERVICE, Sheffield (1990) *Learning Together A, B, C. A Fingerspelling and Alphabet with Signs for Deaf and Hearing Children.* Available from Deaf Advisory Service, Sheffield, c/o Central Deaf Club, 2 Surrey Place, Sheffield S1 2LP.

FULLER, P., GORDON, M. and WRIGHT, P. (1986) *Can Elephants Fly?* Available from the Paget Gorman Society, 3 Gipsy Lane, Headington, Oxford OX3 7PT. (Text with PGSS diagrams.)

HILL, E. (1986) *Where's Spot?* NDCS. Signed language translations by Stephen Iliffe (Signed English).

HILL, E. (1988) *Spot Goes to School.* NDCS. Signed language translations by Stephen Iliffe (Signed English).

MATTIAS, B. and THOMSON, R. (1988) *A to Z Transport.* NDCS (Signed English).

MATTIAS, B. and THOMSON, R. (1988) *A to Z My Body.* NDCS (Signed English).

MATTIAS, B. and THOMSON, R. (1988) *A to Z Food.* NDCS (Signed English).

MATTIAS, B. and THOMSON, R. (1988). *A to Z Animals.* NDCS (Signed English).

MATTIAS, B. and THOMSON, R. (1990) *A to Z Christmas.* NDCS (Signed English).

The NDCS have an up-to-date list of sign language resource material.

Books for Children Relating to Hearing Impairment

BRUNA, D. and JONES, P. (1984) *Blue Boat.* Methuen Children's Books.

SNELL, N. (1984) *Peter Gets a Hearing Aid.* Althea.

Index

Note: Page references in italics indicate tables and figures; headings in italics indicate case studies.